W9-ACU-798

BUSINESS the

Bill
Gates
Way

BUSINESS the Bill Gates Way

10 Secrets of the World's Richest Business Leader

BY DES DEARLOVE

AMACOM

American Management Association

New York • Atlanta • Boston • Chicago • Kansas City • San Francisco • Washington, D.C.

Brussels • Mexico City • Tokyo • Toronto

This book is available at a special
discount when ordered in bulk quantities.
For information, contact Special Sales Department,
AMACOM, an imprint of AMA Publications, a division of
American Management Association,
1601 Broadway, New York, NY 10019.

Business the Bill Gates Way was written independently by the author, Des Dearlove. It has not been authorized by its subject.

This publication is designed to provide accurate and authoritative information in regard to the subject matter covered. It is sold with the understanding that the publisher is not engaged in rendering legal, accounting, or other professional service. If legal advice or other expert assistance is required, the services of a competent professional person should be sought.

Library of Congress Cataloging-in-Publication Data
Dearlove, Des.
    Business the Bill Gates way : ten secrets of the world's richest
business leader / Des Dearlove.
        p.   cm.
    Includes bibliographic references and index.
    ISBN 0-8144-7036-X
    1. Gates, Bill, 1955-   2. Microsoft Corporation—Management.
3. Entrepeneurship—United States.   4. Success in business—United
States.   I. Title.
HD9696.2.U62G374   1999
658—dc21   98-52524
                                                                          CIP

*Published in North America by arrangement with Capstone
Publishing Limited, Oxford, United Kingdom.*

Printing number

10   9   8   7   6   5   4   3   2   1

Contents

Acknowledgments

I'd like to think this is a fair analysis of why Bill Gates has been so successful over so many years. In the end though, whether you see him as the Antichrist or the Messiah, it is impossible to escape the conclusion that he is a remarkable individual. For two decades he has dominated the computer industry.

I would particularly like to thank Randall E. Stross, James Wallace and Jim Erickson for their outstanding books on Microsoft, which were an inspiration.

I would also like to thank Stephen Coomber for his research and insights; and Mark Allin, Richard Burton and Catherine Meyrick at Capstone Publishing.

Des Dearlove
September 1998

Preface

The management gurus tell us that in the contemporary business world learning is a source of competitive advantage. Managers must constantly learn new skills and techniques so that they are armed for corporate battle. Organizations must reinvent themselves as learning organizations in which learning is central to their being and culture. All this is no doubt true—in theory. But, in reality, there are few genuine learning organizations. The reality is that executives are not very good at learning. "Success in the marketplace increasingly depends on learning, yet most people don't know how to learn. What's more, those members of the organization that many assume to be the best at learning are, in fact, not very good at it," says Harvard Business School's Chris Argyris.[1] One of the aims of the Business Way series is to help executives learn by giving them the opportunity to learn from the best.

This may sound like an overly ambitious objective. But think

"Success in the marketplace increasingly depends on learning, yet most people don't know how to learn."

how managers learn. First, they do so through experience. Yet, as Chris Argyris has pointed out, experience is no guarantee of learning. How many executives have you met who have all the experience in the world but little insight or real wisdom? They may proclaim that they have 30 years' experience, but they often have one year's experience 30 times. Experience does not automatically lead to learning. Years clocked up do not necessarily equate with wisdom.

The second source of learning for executives is training programs. Most senior managers have attended one business school executive program or another.

With their case studies and emphasis on the analytical, business schools undoubtedly enable managers to acquire important skills. But the range of skills and their practical usefulness is regularly questioned—not least by those who teach at business schools. "The idea that you can take smart but inexperienced 25-year-olds who have never managed anything or anybody and turn them into effective managers via two years of classroom training is ludicrous," says strategy guru Henry Mintzberg.[2]

The venerable Peter Drucker is another long-time critic of business schools. "The business schools in the U.S., set up less than a century ago, have been preparing well-trained clerks," he wrote as long ago as 1969.[3] More recently, he has predicted the decline of business schools, noting that, "Business schools are suffering from premature success. Now, they are improving yesterday a little bit. The worst thing is to improve what shouldn't be done at all."

Business schools remain wedded to theory; business is about action. "I am not impressed by diplomas. They don't do the work. My marks were not as good as those of others, and I didn't take the final examination. The principal called me in and said I have to leave. I told him that I didn't want a diploma. They had less value than a cinema ticket. A ticket at least guaranteed that you would get in. A diploma guaranteed nothing," said Soichiro Honda, founder of Honda.[4]

Business schools remain wedded to theory; business is about action.

With surprising understatement, former Chrysler CEO Lee Iacocca noted: "Formal learning can teach you a great deal, but many of the essential skills in life are the ones you have to develop on your own." More opinionated was the late Avis chief and author of *Up the Organization*, Robert Townsend. "Don't hire Harvard Business School graduates," he warned. "This elite, in my opinion, is missing some pretty fundamental requirements for success: humility; respect for people in the firing line; deep understanding of the nature of the business and the kind of people who can enjoy themselves making it prosper; respect from way down the line; a demonstrated record of guts, industry, loyalty down, judgment, fairness, and honesty under pressure."[5]

More recently Bill Gates, Virgin's Richard Branson and Body Shop's Anita Roddick have all been much quoted examples of those who missed out on business school but went on to reach the summits of business success. "A great advantage I had when I started the Body Shop was that I had never been to business school," says Anita Roddick. Similarly, 1-800-Flowers founder Jim McCann says that the company would have not got off the ground if he'd gone to business school. "I would have thought too much about why the deal couldn't be done," says McCann.[6]

The third source of learning is learning from peers and colleagues. This is very powerful. The current trend for mentoring and coaching is evidence that senior managers can play an important role in developing the skills of other, more junior, managers. But, what if your boss is an ineffective time-server with no interest in developing tomorrow's talent? What if your boss is incompetent? What if your aspirations far outstrip the level of expertise of your boss? Whom do you learn from then?

For many, the answer lies in the growing array of best-selling books by corporate leaders. Executives buy them by the millions. They want to know what makes a top CEO tick. They want it mapped out. Invariably they are disappointed. Most CEO-authored books are marred by ego and hindsight. They are ghostwritten and their merit is as illusory as a ghost. Most are rose-tinted celebrations of careers rather than objective examinations of managerial techniques. The learning they offer is limited, though that is not to deny the entertainment value.

The Business Way series aims to fill the gap. It seeks to give an objective view of the business practice and thinking of some of the corporate greats. For each of the business

"Guru? You find a gem here or there. But most of it's fairly obvious, you know."

leaders in the series—whether it be Bill Gates, Rupert Murdoch, Richard Branson, or Jack Welch—we look at the essence of their approach to business. What makes them different? What are they good at? And, most importantly, what lessons can be learned from their business success?

As you will see, the lessons aren't rocket science. Indeed, management is more pocket science. "Guru? You find a gem here or there. But most of it's fairly obvious, you know," says Rupert Murdoch. "You go to Doubleday's business section and you see all those wonderful titles and you spend $300 and then you throw them all away." Theory is for those with time on their hands. Making it happen is what management and business are all about. Ask Bill Gates.

NOTES

1 Argyris, Chris, "Teaching smart people how to learn," *Harvard Business Review*, May–June 1991.

2 Mintzberg, Henry, "The new management mind-set," *Leader to Leader*, Spring 1997.

3 Drucker, Peter, *The Age of Discontinuity*, Heinemann, London, 1969.

4 Crainer, Stuart (editor), *The Ultimate Book of Business Quotations*, Capstone, Oxford, 1997; AMACOM, New York, 1998.

5 Townsend, Robert, *Up the Organization* (out of print).

6 Bruce, Katherine, "How to succeed in business without an MBA," *Forbes*, January 26, 1998.

BUSINESS the *Bill Gates* Way

The Life and Times of Bill Gates

THE GATES PHENOMENON

At 43, Bill Gates is the richest man in the world. He has headed Microsoft since he was 20. Believed to be worth something in the region of $50 billion (although Gates himself insists that much of his money is tied up in Microsoft shares), his is wealth of a magnitude that is beyond the comprehension of most people. For this reason he attracts both our envy and our curiosity.

Gates is a twentieth-century phenomenon: the greatest of the cyber-tycoons. It has become a popular pastime in bars and restaurants to astound friends and acquaintances with calculations of his spending power. It is tempting to believe that there has never been another business leader so loaded. In fact, there have been other mega-rich businesspeople, Henry Ford and John D. Rockefeller to name just two. But Gates' wealth is only part of his fascination.

Gates' meteoric rise to fame and fortune confirms the creation of a new business world order, one that is dominated by a different class of entrepreneur and business leader. We may like to label them nerds, but they know things that most of us don't. They understand the potential of the new technology in a way that the traditional generalist manager and bean-counting accountant can't hope to. They are smart—very, very smart—about stuff we don't really understand, and it makes the rest of us uncomfortable.

When it comes to the future, they "get it," and we don't. Technically literate and intellectually elitist, Gates is a sign of the leaders to come. Although he is based at Redmond, Washington, he is probably the greatest of what we can term the Silicon Valley entrepreneurs. To some in Microsoft, he is a mystical, almost religious figure, while to others in the industry he is the Antichrist. Both views are outrageous, but underline just how powerful his influence is. (With all the hullabaloo about alleged abuse of monopoly power, it is easy to forget that back in the 1970s IBM, too, was the target of antitrust investigations. Yet memory fades. Today, we have come to regard Big Blue as almost saintly compared to Microsoft. Such is the nature of power—we fear most what we understand least.)

You won't find any clues to the Gates management technique or leadership style in business schools. In fact, the management professors and gurus are strangely silent on what makes the Microsoft chairman and CEO so successful. Perhaps they feel slighted. Gates, after all, dropped out of Harvard where he was majoring in law. The academics prefer more conventional business leaders—the traditional company executives.

Where, then, should we turn for an insight into what makes this remarkable man tick? Where better than Microsoft's own encyclopedia, *Encarta*? "Much of Gate's success rests on his ability to translate technical visions into market strategy and to blend creativity with technical acumen," it says under the entry for Gates, William, Henry, III. In the end, what sets Bill Gates apart from any other business leader in history is probably the influence that he wields over our lives. Whereas the power of earlier tycoons was usually concentrated in one sector or industry, through the power of software, Microsoft extends its tentacles into every sphere of our lives.

Media barons like Rupert Murdoch make us uneasy because they have the power to control what appears in our newspapers and television screen. But the influence of the people who write software is incalculable. *Encarta*, the encyclopedia produced by Microsoft, is just one example among many of how Bill Gates and his company pervade every aspect of our lives. No wonder we feel uncomfortable with his domination of the software market. No wonder he is vilified and attacked. After all, how many business leaders get the chance to rewrite history?

But beneath the hype and counterhype, what sort of man is Bill Gates? Is he some brainy but basically benign computer whiz-kid, who was in the right place at the right time? Or is there something more sinister about a man who could have retired comfortably in his 20s but prefers to carry on working 16-hour days most days? Stories abound about Gates the genius mathematician and computer programmer, and about the other Gates, the ruthless businessman who goes all out to crush the competition. Only by separating the fact from the fiction can we begin to reveal the real Gates. What emerges from this analysis is a far more complicated picture.

This is not simply a story of technical brilliance and enormous wealth. It is one of remarkable business vision and an obsessive desire to win. It is also about a radically different leadership style from anything the business world has seen before. What Bill Gates offers business leaders of the future is a new template, one that brings together characteristics and skills that are much more suited to the challenges of the twenty-first century. With all his faults, Bill Gates has much to teach the next generation of entrepreneurs and executives.

BILL'S BIG IDEA: A COMPUTER ON EVERY DESK AND IN EVERY HOME

Since the early days of Microsoft, Gates has pursued his vision of "a computer on every desk and in every home." (Interestingly, the original slogan was "a computer on every desk in every home, running Microsoft software," but the last part is often left off these days because it makes some people uncomfortable.)

Hindsight is a wonderful thing. Foresight, however, is much more lucrative, as Gates has shown.

Looking back now, the spread of personal computers from the office into the home seems almost inevitable. Hindsight is a wonderful thing. Foresight, however, is much more lucrative, as Gates has shown. It is important to remember, too, that the ubiquitous screens and keyboards that we all take for granted today were the stuff of science fiction just a couple of decades ago. In the 1960s when futurists in America tried to predict the trends that were likely to shape society in the rest of the century, they completely missed the rise of the PC. It is no coincidence either that the young Gates devoured science fiction books.

That Bill Gates alone was responsible for putting the PC in homes and offices all over the world is untrue, any more than Henry Ford was responsible for the rise of the automobile. What the two had in common, however, was the vision to see what was possible and to play a pivotal role in making that vision a reality.

Gates set about achieving his vision by transforming Microsoft into a major player in the computer industry and using its dominant position to create a platform for the huge growth in applications. Gates realized very early on that, in order for his vision to succeed, it was essential that an industry standard be created. He knew, too, that whoever got there first would have a major opportunity to claim authority in the computing industry.

Several years before IBM approached Gates to find an operating system for its new PC, Gates was lamenting the lack of a common platform and predicting that without one the potential of PCs would not be realized. Articles he penned at that time suggest that he has no more idea of the role destiny had in mind for him than anyone else. The fact is, however, when the opportunity presented itself, Gates saw it for what it was and grabbed it with both hands. He's been doing much the same ever since.

In the early 1980s, Gates masterminded Microsoft's movement from a developer of programming languages to a diversified software company, producing everything from operating systems such as Windows to applications like Word and Excel, as well as programming tools. In the process he transformed the computer industry.

Those who like to criticize him and accuse him of monopolistic tendencies might pause once in a while to reflect on where the PC revolution would be right now without the timely, if self-interested, intervention of Bill Gates. In the end, for all his faults, it's hard to argue with the claim that Bill Gates played a major role in ushering in a new technological era. It's worth remembering, too, that unlike many of the world's seriously rich people, he still works for a living.

THE GEEKS SHALL INHERIT THE EARTH

Gates is one of the few founding CEOs from the technical side of the PC industry who has survived and thrived on the business side. He is a bona fide computer nerd.

William Henry Gates III was born in Seattle, Washington, on October 28, 1955. His parents nicknamed him "Trey" from the III in his name and members of the family never called him anything else. Gates had a precocious intellect—he read the family's encyclopedia from beginning to end at the age of eight or nine. (His company, Microsoft, would later publish the first CD-ROM encyclopedia in the world, *Encarta*). But his real gift was for mathematics, at which he excelled.

Young Bill was already fascinated with computers by the age of 12 and, with his long-time business partner and friend Paul Allen, was involved with various programming projects throughout high school. With Allen he would later to set up Microsoft.

A brilliant student, unlike most gifted children Gates seems to have excelled at everything he did. His passion for winning also seems to have been apparent from an early age. At Lakeside, the elitist Seattle private school that attracts some of the brightest students on America's West Coast, his love of mathematics became an obsession with computers. Even at Lakeside, Bill Gates stood out. He was teased by the other kids because he was clearly so much brighter than the other students.

As James Wallace and Jim Erikson note in their book *Hard Drive*: "Even in an environment like Lakeside, where smart kids tended to command respect, anyone as smart as Gates got teased by some of the others."[1]

According to one classmate who is now a prominent Seattle architect: "Gates most associated with the kids in the computer room. He was socially inept and uncomfortable around others. The guy was totally obsessed with his interest in computers … You would see him playing tennis occasionally, but not much else. Initially, I was in awe of Gates and the others in the computer room. I even idolized them to some extent. But I found that they were such turkeys that I didn't want to be around them. They were part of the reason I got out of computer work … They had developed very narrowly socially and they were arrogant, and I just didn't want to be like that."[2]

Sour grapes? Perhaps. But clearly Gates and his cronies were exceptional even by Lakeside standards.

By his junior year, Gates was something of a computer guru to the younger Lakeside hackers. He would often hold court in the computer room for hours, telling stories about infamous computer hackers.

Gates and some of his computer friends formed the Lakeside Programmers Group, which was dedicated to finding money-making opportunities to use their new-found computer programming skills. Already a pattern was emerging. As Gates observed later: "I was the mover. I was the guy who said 'Let's call the real world and try to sell something to it.'" He was 13 years old at the time.

The remarkable technical rapport with Allen, two years his senior, seems to have developed at this time. Allen's role in the Microsoft story, and that of a small coterie of Lakesiders recruited by the company, is often understated. Gates, Allen, Kent Evans and Richard Weiland—two other members of the Lakeside Programmers Group—would often spend the whole night hooked up, first to a minicomputer owned by General Electric, and later to one at the Computer Centre Corporation, sometimes not getting home until the early hours.

So consumed was the young Gates that his parents became worried about their son's new hobby. For a time, they put a stop to his activities, fearing that it was affecting his studies. Gates abstained from computers for almost a whole year. Typical of his insatiable hunger for knowledge, he turned his attention to other subjects. In this period, he read a number of biographies, including those of Napoleon and Franklin Roosevelt. He wanted, he said, to understand how the great figures of history thought. He also read business books, science books and novels. One of his favorites was *Catcher in the Rye,* and he would later recite long extracts of the book to his girlfriends. Holden Caulfield, the main character, became one of his heroes.

For the time being, however, any plans young Bill might have for forming a software company with his high school friend and fellow hacker were put on hold. His parents insisted that he should go to college; they felt it would be good for him to mix with other students.

Gates' high IQ and massive personal drive ensured him a place at Harvard University. He arrived at America's most respected seat of learning in Cambridge, Massachusetts in the fall of 1973 with no real sense of direction.

Later, he would say that he went to Harvard to learn from people smarter than he was … and was disappointed.[3] The comment probably says as much about Bill Gates opinion of himself as it does about Harvard.

Listing his academic major as pre-law, Gates might have been expected to follow in the footsteps of his lawyer father. In reality, however, he had little interest in a career in law, and his parents had little doubt that their headstrong son would steer his own course. In their wildest dreams, however, none of them could have imagined just what a meteoric journey it would be.

As it turned out, a degree from Harvard was not in the cards. In 1975, while still at the university, Gates teamed up with Paul Allen once more to develop a version of BASIC, an early computer language. Fired up with the new world at his fingertips, in 1977 Gates decided to drop out of Harvard to work full-time at a small computer software company he had founded with his friend. The company was called Microsoft.

FROM HARVARD DROPOUT
TO COMPUTER ICON

The rise of Microsoft has been both rapid and relentless. Gates soon proved that he combined both a bone-deep technical understanding with superb commercial instincts. When ill health forced Allen to leave Microsoft in the early 1980s, Gates' position as leader was confirmed. In the second half of the 1980s, Microsoft became the darling of Wall Street. From a share price of $2 in 1986, Microsoft stock soared to $105 by first half of 1996, making Gates a billionaire and many of his colleagues millionaires.

Gates and Microsoft are largely inseparable.

But the rise in Microsoft's share price also signaled a new business world order. Management guru Tom Peters says the world changed when the market valuation of Microsoft exceeded that of General Motors. During the writing of this book, on September 16, 1998, the market valuation of Microsoft passed that of the mighty GE to become America's biggest company, with a market value of $262 billion. Gates and Microsoft are largely inseparable.

BUSINESS PHILOSOPHY

Microsoft's history is one of almost uninterrupted rapid growth in one of the most competitive industries in the world. Under the leadership of Bill Gates, who founded the company with Paul Allen in 1974, the company has grown from a two-man operation to one that employs more than 20,500 people and generates in excess of $8.8 billion a year in sales.

Microsoft attributes its success to five factors:

- a long-term approach;
- results orientation;
- teamwork and individual drive;
- a passion for its products and customers; and
- continuous customer feedback.

The company hires very bright, creative people and retains them through a combination of excitement, constant challenge, and excellent working conditions. (The odd stock option helps too.) At less than eight percent, its labor turnover is extremely low for the IT industry.

A relaxed, collegiate style and dislike of status symbols is balanced by a demanding attitude toward performance and meeting deadlines. When people leave, Microsoft's research suggests, they do so because the challenge has run out. But perhaps the most telling test of the Microsoft culture is that so many of the original employees are still there. A lot of people in their late 20s and early 30s have become millionaires by taking advantage of the company's stock options. They could easily retire, but they don't.

As one Microsoft manager puts it: "What else would they do with their lives? Where else could they have so much fun?"

SECRETS OF SUCCESS

Careful analysis reveals ten secrets that explain the success of Microsoft and its remarkable CEO. The secrets of doing business the Bill Gates way are:

1. **Be in the right place at the right time.** It's easy to put Microsoft's success down to one extraordinary piece of good luck—securing the contract to supply IBM with the operating system for its first PC. But there is more to his luck than meets the eye. Gates recognized the significance of the IBM deal. He knew that it could change the history of personal computing, and he worked tirelessly for more than six months to maximize his chance of "being lucky."

2. **Fall in love with the technology.** One of the most important aspects of Microsoft's continued success has been Gates' technological knowledge. He retains control over key decisions in this area. On many occasions he has seen the future direction of technology more clearly than his rivals. He has also been prepared to lead the way.

3. **Take no prisoners.** Gates is a fierce competitor. In everything he does, he is driven to win. As a deal maker this makes him an extremely tough negotiator. He makes no bones about this and talks openly about crushing competitors.

4. **Hire very smart people.** "High-IQ people" is a Microsoft term for the very brightest people. From the start, Gates has always insisted that the company required the very best minds. He does not suffer technological fools gladly. In some quarters this has been seen as elitist and has provoked criticism. But it has a number of positive effects. The company is able to recruit many brilliant students straight from college who are attracted by the prospect of working with the very best.

5. **Learn to survive.** Gates freely admits that most of his commercial battles with competitors have

been lost by them through their own mistakes. What he is especially good at is avoiding the bear traps that others fall into, while exploiting the opportunities that arise from the mistakes of others.

6. **Don't expect any thanks.** Bill Gates knows the importance of having friends in high places. Despite his ongoing battle with the U.S. antitrust regulators, Gates has courted the CEOs of Fortune 500 companies, holding CEO forums in Seattle and other cities across the U.S.

7. **Assume the visionary position.** Bill Gates is a new type of business leader. Over the years, he has repeatedly shown that he is a the closest thing the computer industry has to a seer. His in-depth understanding of technology as a unique way of synthesizing data gives him a special ability to spot future trends and steer Microsoft's strategy. This also inspires awe among Microsoft fans and intimidates its competitors.

8. **Cover all the bases.** A key element of Microsoft's success is its ability to manage a large number of projects simultaneously. Gates himself is the original multitasking person and is said to be able to hold several different technical conversations at the same time. This remarkable ability is reflected in the company's approach. It means that it is constantly exploring new markets and new software applications. This protects it from missing the next "big thing."

9. **Build a byte-sized business.** Relative to its stock market valuation, Microsoft remains a relatively small company. Internally, too, the company is constantly splitting into smaller units to maintain

the optimal entrepreneurial team environment. At times, change has been so rapid that Microsoft seems to be creating new divisions on an almost weekly basis. Gates also relies on maintaining a simple structure to enable him to keep his grip on the company. Whenever he feels that lines of communication are becoming stretched or fuzzy, he has no hesitation in simplifying the structure.

10. **Never, ever take your eye off the ball.** Gates has been at the top of his profession for more than two decades now. In that time he has become the richest man in the world—not bad for someone still in his early 40s. Yet despite his enormous wealth and achievements, Gates shows no signs of slowing down. He says he is driven by a "latent fear" that he might miss the next big thing. He has no intention of repeating the mistakes of other dominant computer companies such as IBM and Apple.

NOTES

1   Wallace, James and Erickson, Jim, *Hard Drive: Bill Gates and the Making of the Microsoft Empire*, John Wiley, New York, 1992.

2   Wallace, James and Erickson, Jim, *Hard Drive: Bill Gates and the Making of the Microsoft Empire*.

3   Wallace, James and Erickson, Jim, *Hard Drive: Bill Gates and the Making of the Microsoft Empire*.

1

Be in the Right Place at the Right Time

The nerds have won.

TOM PETERS, MANAGEMENT WRITER

The position of power that Microsoft enjoys today is the culmination of a business strategy that Bill Gates and his partner Paul Allen formulated many years ago when both were still in their 20s. The key to that success resides in a combination of factors. These include the dazzling technical brilliance of the early Microsoft programmers; the enormous energy and ferocious competitiveness of Gates himself; and his unique vision of how the PC revolution could be brought about and the role Microsoft could play in it.

It's easy to put Microsoft's success down to one extraordinary piece of good luck—securing the contract to supply IBM with the operating system for its first PC. But there was more than just luck involved. Bill Gates recognized the significance of the deal. He knew that an operating system providing a common platform could change the history of personal computing. He worked tirelessly for more than six months to ensure that the opportunity, when it came, would fall to Microsoft. In this way he gave luck a helping hand.

When Gates was preparing to pitch for the IBM contract he is said to have told his mother that she would not see him for six months. During this time he virtually lived at the office, devoting himself entirely to winning the IBM business. He sensed how important it was.

The main competitor for the deal was a company called Digital Research Inc., which owned the operating system that ran the Apple II, the most successful desktop computer. At a crucial stage of the negotiations, however, the key contact at Digital Research was away on vacation for a month. Gates, who viewed taking vacations as a sign of weakness, made sure he capitalized on his competitor's absence.

NERD POWER

From the cradle of the digital revolution, a new kind of business leader was emerging. The nerds were coming and Bill Gates was leading the charge. Gates is the ultimate expression of "nerd power." His own rise to fame and fortune personifies a change in the business constellation. Once unfashionable in corporate America, in the wake of the computer revolution the technical experts—or techies—have risen to prominence.

For the first time ever, perhaps, a high level of technical understanding was essential to understand the strategic possibilities that the brave new world of information technology opened up. The traditional generalist executives were out of their depth. Many still can't even operate the computers on their desks, let alone program one. The new entrepreneurs of Silicon Valley didn't wear suits.

The blue-suited IBMers who had dominated the computer business for decades were suddenly wrong-footed by the switch from mainframes to personal computers. Standing on the threshold of the change was Bill Gates, ready to usher in the new paradigm. But Gates and Paul Allen, his high school friend and partner in computer language development, were very different from the IBMers.

The young Gates, with his bottle-glass spectacles, dandruff and acne, and Allen, with his long hair and shaggy beard, provided Americans with a caricature of the nerds they knew at school. More significantly, for the first time corporate America's discomfort with raw intellect and technical expertise was challenged.

The prevailing myth among the business community of America was that grit, determination, luck and sheer hard graft was enough to get on in business. Brains alone were not seen as the distinguishing factor. In fact, they were sometimes seen as a handicap, especially when they were accompanied by a certain social awkwardness and eccentricity. The new computer whiz-kids flew in the face of the anti-intellectual tradition, according to Randall E. Stross. "The vocabulary might change—eggheads in the 1950s, nerds in the 1970s—but the message is the same: brains are a liability, not an asset."

Until the 1970s, American business heroes were people like Lee Iacocca, the CEO of Chrysler—more John Wayne than Peewee Herman. But suddenly, with the rise of Microsoft and Apple, the nerds were inheriting the business world. The era of nerd power had begun.

Of course the pejorative use of the word *nerd* is an indication of the value society attached to a certain set of characteristics and attitudes—a hangover, in fact, from earlier days when physical prowess and being down-to-earth were regarded as desirable attributes. What we are now experiencing is a shift in values. This is most obvious in the business world, where we are witnessing the rise and rise of the so-called "knowledge worker."

This represents a significant shift in economic power. It has been likened to the change that took place during the industrial revolution when the application of technology in factories altered employment patterns and wealth distribution beyond all recognition. Many experts claim that the onset of the IT revolution represents the most significant change since then. The impact on the corporate world is clear for all to see.

In the era of the knowledge worker, technical know-how and creativity are the new corporate assets. Combine these with business acumen and a highly competitive nature and you have a rare bird indeed. Bill Gates is that rare bird. But a remarkable piece of good fortune carried him to an altitude where his special talents could flourish.

THE DOS BOSS

Bill Gates was in the right place at the right time. At a fateful meeting with IBM in 1980 the future of the entire computer industry—and arguably the entire business world—took an unexpected turn. Executives from Big Blue signed a contract with a small Seattle-based software firm to develop the operating system for its first PC. They thought they were simply saving time by outsourcing a non-core activity to a small contractor. After all, they were in the computer hardware business, where the real money and power lay. But they were wrong. The world was about to change. Unknowingly they were signing over their market leadership position to Bill Gates' Microsoft.

At a fateful meeting with IBM in 1980 the future of the entire computer industry— and arguably the entire business world—took an unexpected turn.

Much has been made of Bill Gates' manipulation of IBM. But the decision was the culmination of a series of mistakes by Big Blue that reflected its complacency at that time. As a result, it frittered away its dominance of the computer industry. One former IBMer likened the culture at Big Blue during that period to the old Soviet bureaucracy, where the way to get ahead was to impress your immediate boss rather than serve the real interests of the people. So it was that a bloated and complacent IBM collided with a hyperactive and hungry Microsoft. The effect was like introducing a fat and sleepy buffalo to a piranha.

Gates was lucky. But had the same opportunity fallen to one of his Silicon Valley peers, the outcome might have been very different. In Bill Gates, IBM had picked the one man who would not fumble the ball. On such moments does history turn. Presented with the chance of a lifetime, Bill Gates would make the most of it. What IBM couldn't see, Gates saw very clearly. The world of computing was on the brink of a major change—what the management theorists like to call a paradigm change. Gates understood in a way that the old IBM guard could not, that software and not hardware was the key to the future. He knew, too, that the muscle of IBM, the market leader, would be required to establish a common standard, or platform, for software applications. That platform would be Q-DOS, an existing operating system that Gates bought from another company and renamed MS-DOS at Microsoft. But even Gates could not have imagined just how lucrative the deal would be for Microsoft.

HOW IBM FUMBLED THE PC MARKET

IBM was late off the mark with the PC. The company that dominated the mainframe computer business failed to recognize the importance of—and the threat presented by—the rise of the personal computer. By the time Big Blue decided to enter the PC market in 1980, Apple, which had pioneered the desktop computer, had become a $100 million business.

Frank Cary, IBM chairman at the time, ordered his people to produce an IBM-badged PC by August 1981. Already in catch-up mode, the IBMers put in charge of the project made two fundamental technical errors. Both mistakes came from a single decision to go outside the company for the two critical elements of the new machine—the microprocessor that would be at the heart of the new PC and the operating system. Intel agreed to supply the chips and a small, relatively unknown software company based in Seattle agreed to supply the operating system.

The launch of the IBM PC was initially a commercial success. But the company ended up giving away most of the profits from its PC business to its two partners. Under the initial contract between IBM and Microsoft, Big Blue agreed to fund most of the development costs of MS-DOS, but only Microsoft was allowed to license the system to third parties. This was the killer clause.

As the PC industry exploded, thousands of new competitors entered the market. Virtually all of them ended up using MS-DOS and paying Bill Gates for the privilege. But IBM's mistakes didn't end there. When it recognized its initial error, IBM failed to renegotiate the licensing contract or to break with Microsoft. Even more mystifying, senior managers at IBM killed an internally developed operating system that could have broken Gate's stranglehold on the PC market.

More than a decade later, IBM was still manufacturing more PCs than any other company, but its personal systems division was losing money. The only companies making large profits in the highly competitive PC business were the suppliers of the micro chips and operating systems. To this day, Intel remains the dominant player in the former and Microsoft in the latter.

STAYING LUCKY

Bill Gates was too bright not to realize that if he played his cards right, his operating system MS-DOS could become the industry standard. At that time, the operating system itself was just one of several on the market.

Many inside the computer industry felt at that time that from a purely technical perspective MS-DOS had some serious drawbacks. Apple was already established as the provider of choice for desk top computers. Apple's founders had brought new attitude and culture to the computer business. Apple's machines were popular because they were simpler to operate and fun to use. The company had yet to develop the famous icon-based Apple Macintosh operating system, but the signs were already there that the people at Apple were ahead of the game.

But Gates had an important ally. He had the muscle of IBM behind his operating system. Big Blue had dominated the mainframe business for years and, somewhat belatedly, was preparing to enter the PC market. The credibility of the IBM name would be crucial in the battle ahead. Gates judged rightly that the best opportunity for establishing an industry standard other than one based around the Apple system lay with the arrival in the PC market of the world's most trusted computer manufacturer. For many years, IBM's proud boast was that "no one ever got fired for buying an IBM." At that time, it had a reputation for dependability unmatched in the computer world. The IBM PC was bound to take a big slice of the market for desktop computers.

Every single PC shipped by IBM would have MS-DOS installed. For Microsoft it was the perfect Trojan horse.

The fact that IBM-badged machines were about to flood the market also meant that the operating system they used would be catapulted into first or second place. Every single PC shipped by IBM would have MS-DOS installed. For Microsoft it was the perfect Trojan horse. Every IBM-badged PC that landed on a desk gave a free ride to the Microsoft operating system that lay hidden inside. This was Bill Gates' amazing piece of luck. But what happened next goes a long way toward explaining why Bill Gates, and not Steve Jobs or some other Silicon Valley entrepreneur, is now the richest man in the world.

By the late 1970s, Microsoft was already licensing its software to a variety of customers. In 1977 Gates supplied software for Tandy, but it also licensed BASIC 6502 to Apple for the Apple II Computer. Microsoft went on to work with many of the other leading computer companies. This suited Bill Gates' purposes perfectly. Microsoft was already beginning to set the industry standard with its software, which was precisely what Gates wanted. It was this strategy that he continued with MS-DOS.

Apple, on the other hand, took the view that the only way to ensure the quality of its products was to try to retain control of everything. Later this included its proprietary Macintosh operating system.

Apple didn't want anyone else to "clone" its computer. For years, the company resolutely refused to license its Apple Mac operating system to other manufacturers. This meant that anyone who wanted the user-friendly Apple operating system had to buy an Apple computer. It was a strategy that seemed to make sense—but only by the old rules of the game. The problem for Apple was that in terms of business model and strategic vision, it was only one generation ahead of the hardware dinosaur IBM.

Apple was in both the hardware and software businesses. Even though its managers recognized the growing value customers attached to the intangible software over the physical hardware, they were unable to divorce the two strategically.

Apple reasoned that they had a killer combination; they reckoned that in the Apple Mac they had the best operating system and the best machine on the market, so it was just a matter of time before they would dominate the desktop industry. The mistake was in believing that the best technology would win in the end. They were wrong. By the time they realized their mistake Gates and Microsoft had seized 80 per cent of the market. (Had Apple's executives taken a look at the development of the VCR some years earlier, they would have realized their mistake. Despite an apparent technological advantage, Sony's Betamax video system was eventually eclipsed by the VHS system.)

The question was whether Gates could go the distance. By the mid-1980s, Gates' reputation as an outstanding programmer was widely accepted. Few doubted that he was one of the most talented techies to emerge from the maelstrom of the Silicon Valley revolution. His competitive spirit and personal drive to succeed were legendary. What critics questioned were his managerial credentials. They asked whether he had the necessary skills and charisma to lead a company that was fast becoming a major player in corporate America.

As early as 1984, *Fortune*[1] magazine chided Gates for failing to develop the management depth to turn the temporary victories he had won into long-term dominance. What the business press had still to learn was that Gates was much more than just a techie or a computer nerd on a lucky streak. There was a lot more to Bill Gates than met the eye. His ascendancy to the corporate throne marked an important shift in the balance of power in the business world.

MOORE'S LAW

In 1965, in what came to be known as Moore's Law, Gordon Moore, a founder of Fairchild Semiconductor and later of Intel, quantified the rate at which micro chips would increase in power. Based on his calculation of the rate at which the technology was advancing, Moore predicted that over the next ten years the number of components that could be fitted on a microchip would continue to double every twelve months.

What this meant, in effect, was that the capability of the chips would double every year without adding significantly to the cost. The prediction proved amazingly accurate. But in the early 1970s few people understood what that would mean for the future of the industry. A couple of computer fanatics from Seattle thought they had a clue.

Moore's law inspired Bill Gates and Paul Allen to set up Microsoft. Gates credits Allen with showing him Moore's Law and pointing out the business potential in exponentially improving semiconductor technology. "Exponential phenomena are rare," Gates recalls asking Allen skeptically. "Are you serious?"

Allen was deadly serious. What he and Gates understood that IBM and DEC didn't was the implications of this. Based on Moore's Law, the two reasoned that if Moore was right then processing power would make microcomputers viable in a very short space of time. "It's going to happen," they said, and they set about preparing to write software for the machines that would follow.

SETTING THE STANDARD

The decision to outsource the operating system to Microsoft was a mistake that cost IBM dearly. Similarly, Apple's decision not to license its operating system was one that subsequently prevented it from taking a larger market share and almost bankrupted the company. These were mistakes that Bill Gates had no intention of repeating.

To this day, those two fateful decisions are ingrained in the Microsoft culture. Most important is the awareness that the company that establishes the industry standard will almost always dominate the market. It is a point hammered home to those who work for Bill Gates.

"We set the standard," was the Microsoft slogan even before it signed the deal with IBM. It underlines the clarity of Gates' thinking from the very beginning. It explains his obsession with bringing new products to market first. When someone gets the jump on Gates, it also explains the ferocity with which Microsoft markets its own version when it comes out. In some cases, too, Gates will simply buy a software company lock, stock and barrel if he believes it has established a significant technological lead on his own company with an important application. In doing so, he ensures that Microsoft will dominate that market from the outset. At the same time, he is able to acquire the technological know-how by bringing the brains behind it into the Microsoft fold.

Today, "We set the standard" remains at the heart of the Bill Gates business strategy. It also provides a timely reminder to anyone at Microsoft who might forget the importance of the IBM lesson.

UBIQUISOFT

Love him or loathe him, the fact is that Bill Gates' Microsoft software dominates the global computer industry. Around 80 percent of all desktop computers run one or other version of Microsoft's Windows software. Moreover, the vast majority of new PCs are shipped with Microsoft software installed. This gives Bill Gates an enormous head start on his rivals.

Around 80 percent of all desktop computers run one or other version of Microsoft's Windows software.

In recent years, Gates has shown that he is adept at leveraging Microsoft's dominant position to capture new and emerging application markets. Some say that he has used what amounts to a stranglehold on the PC software market to foist Microsoft products onto customers. On the other hand, Gates is simply doing what any smart businessperson would do: pressing home the advantage.

It is tempting, perhaps, to look back at the history of personal computing and regard Microsoft's current dominant market position as a given. To do so, though, is to view the PC revolution through a narrow lens; to assume that the market for PCs would have automatically taken off regardless of the actions of key players such as Bill Gates. This would be assuming too much. An alternative interpretation is to look at Microsoft's domination as the result of the mistakes of others—principally IBM and Apple. But this, too, is seriously to underestimate the role of Bill Gates and his colleagues at Microsoft.

NOTE

1   Stross, Randall, E., *The Microsoft Way*, Addison-Wesley, 1996.

BE IN THE RIGHT PLACE
AT THE RIGHT TIME

In the era of the knowledge worker, technical know-how and creativity are the new corporate assets. Combine these with business acumen and a highly competitive nature and you have a rare bird indeed. Bill Gates is that rare bird. But a remarkable piece of good fortune carried him to an altitude where his special talents could flourish. The first lessons from the Bill Gates school of business leadership are:

♦ *Be in the right place at the right time. Microsoft had a huge dollop of luck in 1980 when IBM, then the market leader in the computer industry, signed a contract with Bill Gates to develop the operating system for its first PC.*

♦ *Stay lucky—don't fumble the ball. Being lucky only gets you so far; it's what you do with that luck that really counts. There are a great many millionaires in Silicon Valley who might have been billionaires if they had exploited their good fortune as Gates has. When the opportunity of a lifetime dropped into his arms, Gates grabbed it with both hands. He's been scoring touchdowns ever since, and shows no signs of relinquishing possession of the ball.*

♦ *He who sets the standard wins. What Gates understood that others did not was that in the computer business, market share is self-perpetuating. Once a company establishes an industry standard it becomes much harder for a newcomer to usurp its position. "We set the standard" has been the Microsoft motto since its early days, long before it signed the fateful contract with IBM. Today it remains at the heart of Bill Gates' business strategy.*

♦ *Leverage your bits off. Gates has successfully leveraged Microsoft's dominant market position to establish its own versions of new applications. It is this aggressive marketing strategy that has prompted the U.S. government's antimonopoly authorities to investigate the software giant.*

♦ *Let the technology shape your strategy. Gates is one of the few business leaders who really understands the technology. This enables him to make strategic decisions based on his own vision of where the technology is heading.*

Fall in Love with the Technology

*I actually understand how to write software;
there's a whole new world of standards to be
developed; my people are smarter about this
stuff and nobody else is doing it.*

BILL GATES

B ill Gates has had a lifelong love affair with the personal computer. From the very beginning, Gates and his partner Paul Allen could see that the PC would change everything. The two would talk late into the night about what the post-PC world would be like. They never truly doubted that the revolution would come. "It's going to happen" was an article of faith for the fledgling Microsoft, and they were going to write software for it when it did. What neither could have imagined then was the part that they would play or the extraordinary turn of events that would catapult their company onto the world stage. But even then they knew what IBM and other mainframe computer

"I remember from the very beginning, we wondered, 'What would it mean for DEC once microcomputers were powerful and cheap enough? What would it mean for IBM?' To us it seemed they were screwed."

companies such as Digital Equipment Corporation didn't—that they were in deep, deep trouble.

"I remember from the very beginning, we wondered, 'What would it mean for DEC once microcomputers were powerful and cheap enough? What would it mean for IBM?' To us it seemed they were screwed. We thought maybe they'd even be screwed tomorrow. We were saying God, how come these guys aren't stunned? How come they're not just amazed and scared?"[1]

Gates' technological knowledge is one of the most important factors in Microsoft's continued success. He retains control over key decisions in this area. On many occasions he has seen the future direction of technology more clearly than his rivals.

CODE WARRIORS

Gates is one of the few founding CEOs from the technical side of the PC industry who has survived and thrived on the business side. His love affair with the technology gives his leadership a distinctive edge. For all his wealth and commercial experience, deep down Gates remains what he was at the start—a techie.

Gates regards "writing code"—as computer programming is known—as a higher calling. Employees at Microsoft are divided into two classes: product development groups, which include the top programmers; and everyone else.

The product groups receive the lion's share of the stock options; their programmers' private offices at the Microsoft campus at Redmond are defended most vigorously whenever there is a shortage of office space. (Eventually the squeeze became so intense that in

1995 smaller product groups were moved into an annex about a mile away from the main campus.)

Colleagues at Microsoft agree that Gates' technical knowledge gives him an edge. "He has the ability to ask the right question. He'll know some intricate detail about a program and you wonder, 'How does he know that?'" says Brad Silverberg, who was part of the Windows development team.

Gates himself claims to be able to recall "huge slabs" of code many years after he has last tinkered with it. In the old days, he would personally review every line of code. That is no longer possible, although he still takes a keen interest in all new Microsoft products.

"I'm certainly able to use all the products we have," he says, "but I can't possibly review all the code. My role is more to do with the strategy and the direction people are moving in and how well they work together. There's a lot of invention going on and I have to pick which things are important and express them to the user. It's all very critical."

Business, on the other hand, requires no special expertise, in Gates' view. "If you're any good at math at all, you understand business—it's not its own deep, deep subject," he said in 1992. It required just 10 percent of his own "mental cycle," he said.

Gates on business know-how:

"If you're any good at math at all, you understand business—it's not its own deep, deep subject."

START YOUNG

Gates' preference for hiring the brightest graduates straight out of college is well known. At first, the company simply hired clever people Gates and his partner Paul Allen knew from school. These they called "smart friends." But by the time Microsoft moved from Albuquerque to Seattle it had run out of smart friends and had to start recruiting "smart strangers."

Over the years, the company has developed its own special recruitment techniques and preferences. From the very beginning, Gates recognized that his approach to developing software could best be nurtured among "very young people, fairly inexperienced."

So when by 1994 the average age of Microsoft employees had risen to 31, Gates confessed that he would like to see the percentage of employees hired direct from college return to the 80 percent it had been in the early years. "Young people are more willing to learn, and come up with new ideas," he said.[2]

Gates' own love affair with computers began when he was in high school. At that time, few schools could afford to provide their students with access to a computer, but Lakeside, the school he attended, was an exception. Gates made his first deal in the computer business at the tender age of 13 when he agreed to look for software bugs in return for free computer time. "I was lucky enough when I was quite young to have an exposure to computers, which were very expensive and kind of limited in what they could do, but still they were fascinating."

For the young Gates, the discovery of computers opened up a whole new world. What he and his teenage friends could see that adults already working in the computer industry could not was the enormous potential of the computer to change people's lives. The prevailing logic at that time was that computers belonged in offices and would remain there. But to Gates and his friends, the potential was much greater.

"Some friends of mine and I talked about that a lot and decided that, because of the miracle of chip technology, they would change into something that everybody could use. We didn't see any limit to the computer's potential, and we really thought writing software was a neat thing. So we hired our friends who wrote software to see what kind of a tool this could really be—a tool for the Information Age that could magnify your brainpower instead of just your muscle power."

The other great advantage that Bill Gates and his Microsoft cronies had was that they were involved with the development of personal computing from its earliest days. "By pursuing that with a pretty incredible focus and by being there at the very beginning of the industry, we were able to build a company that has played a very central role in what's been a pretty big revolution. Now fortunately, the revolution is still at the beginning. It was 23 years ago when we started the company. But there's no doubt that if we take the habits we formed and stick with them, the next 23 years should give us a lot more potential and maybe even get us pretty close to our original vision—'a computer on every desk and in every home.'"

Their youth also created some problems. When they first set up Microsoft, Gates and his partner Paul Allen had trouble getting other parts of the industry to take them seriously. As Gates explains, "At first you'll run into some skepticism. If you're young, it's hard to go lease premises. You couldn't rent a car when you were under 25, so I was always taking taxis to go see customers. When people would ask me to go have discussions in the bar, well, I couldn't go to the bar."

But youth also had its advantages. For one thing, it meant that Gates' business acumen was often underestimated in the early days. As Jack Sams, one of the IBM executives who signed the contract with the 21-year-old Gates to supply the operating system for the first IBM PC, recalls: "When he came out, I thought he was the office boy."

It was a mistake that IBM would regret. Gates was aware of the impression that his youth created, and used it to good advantage.

"That's fun," he observed years later, "because when people are first skeptical, they say, 'Oh, this kid doesn't know anything.' But when you show them you've really got a good product and you know something, they actually tend to go overboard. So, at least in this country, our youth was a huge asset for us once we reached a certain threshold."

GEEK CHIC

What the socially awkward Gates also achieved at Microsoft was to make software development fashionable for the first time. In part, this was simply the result of the large sums of money that could be earned from developing good products. But it went further. When Gates and his Lakeside friends had first started hanging out in the school's computer room, they were regarded as geeks. Then as companies such as Microsoft and rival Apple became better known, public perception started to change.

By the mid-1980s it was "cool" to be into computers. Throughout America, the brightest college students had a new career in mind. They couldn't wait to finish school to get out to Silicon Valley or the Microsoft campus at Redmond, where things were really happening.

By the mid-1980s it was "cool" to be into computers.

Throughout America, the brightest college students had a new career in mind. They couldn't wait to finish school to get out to Silicon Valley or the Microsoft campus at Redmond, where things were really happening. Microsoft had its own special hip culture and slant on the business.

By then, Gates and his colleagues at Microsoft had invented their own language, based on slang they used as schoolyard computer hackers. Examples include:

- Dogfood—what Microsoft programmers call flawed software; software that's not good enough for sale but good enough for internal use.
- Selftoast—to contradict yourself.
- Vaporware—a product that never reached the shelves, for one reason or another.
- Face-mail—having a conversation in the same room (as opposed to voice mail or E-mail).
- Braindump—passing on technical knowledge.

R&D FOREVER

Coming from the technical side as he does, Bill Gates understands the importance of investing in research. He invests an extraordinarily high percentage of Microsoft's revenues into research and development. In 1984 *Forbes* magazine, which compiles an annual list of the richest people in the world, observed that Gates would never appear in its annual review of America's richest people, because he poured so much money into R&D.

Coming from the technical side as he does, Bill Gates understands the importance of investing in research. He invests an extraordinarily high percentage of Microsoft's revenues into research and development.

Gates acknowledges that the disproportionately high research budget is one of the main reasons for Microsoft's success, but says it is one that other companies could easily imitate. By pouring huge amounts of the company's revenues into R&D, Gates ensures that Microsoft is always prospecting for the next big thing. While other computer companies have been content to rest on their laurels, Microsoft is developing products in its software laboratories for up to five years down the road.

Microsoft is not the most innovative company in the world, but its ability to take ideas and make them into commercial propositions is second to none. What Bill Gates has demonstrated many times over is that innovation and R&D are not necessarily the same thing. In many cases, the emphasis is on researching how customers want to use an application and developing a marketable product that meets their requirements. Pure innovation, Gates believes, is overrated. He prefers to look around for existing solutions that can be refined, rather than constantly reinventing the wheel.

DON'T REINVENT THE WHEEL

Microsoft's rivals claim that the company is not good at innovation and has a poor track record for creating software from scratch. Mike Zisman of Lotus, a longtime

Microsoft rival, observes: "I don't worry about Microsoft. It never invented anything." But the bravado masks the real strength of the software wizards of Redmond: They are very, very good at taking ideas and turning them into usable products.

In fact, Gates himself is not an original thinker and does not actually admire people who are obsessed with original solutions to problems. Most people have only one brilliant idea in their entire lifetimes, he says.

GM VERSUS MICROSOFT

Management guru Tom Peters points to a day in mid-1992 as the day the world changed.[3] At that moment, the stock market valuation of Microsoft exceeded that of General Motors for the first time. On that day Wall Street put a higher value on Microsoft, which owns virtually no physical assets besides some buildings in Redmond, Washington, than it did on GM, with all its factories, offices and inventory. The idea would have been unthinkable just a few years ago.

By investing so much of the company's revenues in R&D, Gates constantly adds to Microsoft's reservoir of intellectual capital. According to Johan Roos, professor of strategy at the world famous Swiss business school IMD, GM symbolizes the industrial era, whereas Microsoft symbolizes the new era of information.[4]

How can you explain the switch? "The crux," Professor Roos observes, "is that it is individuals who are the chief source of competitive advantage, rather than the physical assets the company owns and controls.

"...Intellectual capital as a concept says more about the future earnings capabilities of a company than any of the conventional performance measurements we currently use," notes Roos. "If the top fifty programmers suddenly left Microsoft, the share price would probably drop dramatically."

"I don't worry about Microsoft. It never invented anything."

He believes that most solutions already exist somewhere and simply have to be identified. This, he claims, is his own great talent—identifying solutions, acquiring them and developing them into commercially successful products.

Even DOS, the operating system that made Microsoft famous, was not invented by Gates. His partner Paul Allen bought a version of an operating system called Q-DOS from another computer company, Seattle Computers, for $50,000. Microsoft developed it and supplied it to IBM for its first PC. Gates and Allen made billions of dollars as a result.

What Microsoft has also shown itself to be good at is shaping the future direction of technology, most noticeably the spread of multimedia. In the early days of CD-ROM, for example, when the technology was having difficulty being accepted, Gates funded a series of conferences to promote the new technology. These events championed the cause of the new technology and placed Microsoft at the center of the CD-ROM movement.

When it still failed to catch on, Gates realized that there was a chicken and egg problem. Hardware manufacturers were not going to include CD-ROM drives on their systems until someone produced some CD-ROM titles users could buy. By the same token, no one wanted to invest in developing CD-ROM titles until the hardware was there to play them. The result was a stalemate that threatened to block the new technology. Gates instructed his developers to create some CD-ROM titles double quick. The result was a series of reference titles that led eventually to the creation of *Encarta*, the first multimedia encyclopedia. CD-ROM, as we all know, took off.

It is his love affair with the computer that keeps Bill Gates at the forefront of his industry, an industry in which you can all too easily lose the plot. "The key point is that you've got to enjoy what you do every day. For me, that's working with very smart people and it's working on new problems. Every time we think, 'Hey, we've had a little bit of success,' we're pretty careful not to dwell on it too much because the bar gets raised. We've always got customer feedback telling us that the machines are too complicated and they're not natural enough. The competition, the technological breakthroughs and the research make the computer industry, and in particular software, the most exciting field there is, and I think I have the best job in that business."[5]

FALL IN LOVE WITH THE TECHNOLOGY

The second set of lessons from the Bill Gates school of business:

♦ *Understand the technology. In the era of the knowledge worker, it takes a techie to run a company like Microsoft. Only someone with a bone-deep knowledge of the technology can truly understand what's going on in the industry, identify trends, and set strategy.*

♦ *Create a business culture that recognizes the importance of technical experts. Most companies have traditionally valued generalists more highly than specialists. At Microsoft the software developers are regarded as more important than managers.*

♦ *Start young. Gates' love affair with computers began when he was in high school. At that time, few schools could afford to provide their students with access to a computer, but Lakeside, the school Gates attended, was an exception. Gates made his first deal in the computer business at the tender age of 13 when he agreed to look for software bugs in return for free computer time.*

♦ *Invest more than anyone else. By pouring huge amounts of the company's revenues into R&D, Gates ensures that Microsoft is always prospecting for the next big thing. While other computer companies have been content to rest on their laurels, Microsoft is developing products in its software laboratories for up to five years down the road.*

♦ *Lead technology to shape the future. Although Microsoft is not a prodigious inventor, it is extremely good at taking good ideas, developing them and making them into commercially successful products. In fact, Gates himself is not an original thinker and does not actually admire people who are obsessed with original solutions to problems. Most people have only one brilliant idea in their entire lifetimes, he says. He believes that most solutions already exist somewhere and simply have to be identified. This, he claims, is his own great talent. Gates has also shown himself willing to use Microsoft's muscle to champion new technologies such as multi-media, which then shape the future.*

NOTES

1   Schlender, Brent, "Bill Gates and Paul Allen talk," *Fortune*, October 2, 1995.

2   Stross, Randall E., *The Microsoft Way: the Real Story of How the Company Outsmarts Its Competiton*, Addison-Wesley Longman, Inc., Reading, MA, 1996.

3   Peters, Thomas, *Liberation Management*, Alfred A. Knopf Inc., New York, 1992.

4   Roos, Johan, "Intellectual Capital: what you can measure you can manage," *Perspectives for Managers*, Vol 26, No. 10, IMD, Nov 1996.

5   "The Bill and Warren show," *Fortune*, July 20, 1998.

3

Take No Prisoners

Gates is tenacious. That's what's scary ... he always comes back, like Chinese water torture. His form of entertainment is tearing people to shreds.

STEWART ALSOP, EDITOR OF *PC LETTER*

B ill Gates is a fierce competitor, addicted to winning. This makes him an extremely tough adversary. He makes no bones about this and talks openly about crushing competitors.

The marketing of Microsoft products, including the frequent upgrades that make earlier versions of software obsolete, has ruffled feathers inside the U.S. government. These and other concerns—including a series of complaints from rivals in the computer industry—have aroused the interest of the Federal antitrust authorities, which have investigated Microsoft for alleged anticompetitive practices. No case has yet been proved.

Gates vigorously defends the company's marketing strategy, claiming Microsoft has had a positive impact on consumer choice. Whatever the final outcome of that investigation, no one denies that Gates is a formidable competitor and superb marketing strategist. According to *Fortune* magazine, every successful enterprise requires three people: a dreamer, a businessperson, and a son-of-a-bitch. "Bill Gates has all three qualities, making him stand out as the most successful start-from-nothing businessman the world has ever known."

It is telling that when Gates talks about the competition he lumps them all together. When competitors talk about Gates they single him out.

LEVERAGE YOUR BITS OFF

What Gates is unquestionably good at is leveraging Microsoft's market position to provide access to new and emerging markets. The reality is that if you own the operating system that runs 80 percent of the desktop computers in the world that gives you a lot of negotiating and marketing muscle. Not only does it generate huge amounts of cash to be reinvested in new product research and development, it also provides unique opportunities for the packaging or bundling of software products.

On a number of occasions Gates has used his dominant market position effectively to shut out competitors. He has never been afraid to go to war with a big competitor, as he showed when Apple decided that the takeup of his Windows graphical interface gave him too much power, or later when Apple and IBM joined forces to topple him, or when he fought a database war with Borland.

Such has been his success in these and other turf wars that the smart money in Silicon Valley does not bet against Microsoft.

IF YOU CAN'T BEAT THEM, BUY THEM

Gates' pragmatism also extends to buying his way into key markets. He is quite prepared to go out and buy the development expertise of other companies and then plug it into the Microsoft machine. Faced with a need to create database products to compete with Borland, for example, Gates went out and spent $170 million buying the Foxpro program, software that had already been developed by another company.

In fact, this is a strategy that Gates has used many times. In 1982, for example, he bought the basis of DOS from a small company called Seattle Computers, and went on to make it into the industry standard. And it's not just software that he's prepared to plunder. On occasions, too, Gates has bought companies simply to acquire the expertise of exceptional programmers, who often have a stake in the smaller firm. In such cases Gates is able to offer several million dollars for the company as an inducement for the key individuals to join Microsoft. In this way he can bring deep seams of technical expertise into Microsoft very rapidly.

"We've bought a lot of small companies, and I'd say that's been vital to us. These are companies that on their own probably wouldn't have made it, but when their abilities are combined with ours, both of us were able to create a much better set of products than we could've otherwise."

SLEEPING WITH THE ENEMY

For all his fighting talk, another characteristic of Bill Gates is that he does not allow grudges to affect his commercial decisions. The ultimate pragmatist, on many occasions Gates has fought a pitched battle with a rival for years, only to turn around and do business with them when it suits him. In almost every case, it is on his terms.

In recent years, for example, he has happily poured money into Apple to shore up the company that had been attacking his market position with Windows.

Whereas many business leaders become locked into aggressive positions, allowing their personal grudges to dictate their decisions, Gates is always rational. Critics claim that he allows his emotions to get the better of him in some cases—in particular, that his dislike of certain rivals has clouded his judgment. There is no proof of this. On the contrary, like a spoiled child who throws a tantrum to get its way, Gates may personalize a battle for a time, but only to focus Microsoft's fire.

In a passionate industry, Gates has a remarkable ability to keep personalities out of business decisions. Whatever he might do—even if it proved ruinous to another company—would be for a purely commercial end. What matters to Gates is winning; in order to do so he will beat the enemy, but that doesn't mean he won't work with them at a later date. This makes him a far more dangerous adversary than someone who is hotheaded or acts out of emotion.

Competing with Bill Gates is like playing a game of chess. He is always thinking many moves ahead and will punish his opponents' blunders with cold-blooded predatory indifference. That's why so many people in the industry fear him.

RISK MANAGEMENT

Along with his analytical and detached approach to business, Gates is also a shrewd judge of risk. This is something he has learned along the way. But while others who are risk averse have a tendency to delay decisions, Gates is only too aware that in the computer industry the speed of change is so rapid that not acting often carries the greatest risk of all. Risk, he knows, has to be balanced against reward.

"If you're going to start a company, it takes so much energy that you'd better overcome your feeling of risk. Also, I don't think that you should necessarily start a company at the beginning of your career. There's a lot to be said for working for a company and learning how they do things first. In our case, Paul Allen and I were afraid somebody else might get there before us. It turned out we probably could've waited another year, in fact, because things were a little slow to start out, but being on the ground floor seemed very important to us.

"I was so excited that I didn't think of it as being all that risky. It's true, I might have gone bankrupt, but I had a set of skills that were highly employable. And my parents were still willing to let me go back to Harvard and finish my education if I wanted to.

Bill Gates on risk management:

"If you're going to start a company, it takes so much energy that you'd better overcome your feeling of risk."

"The thing that was scary to me was when I started hiring my friends, and they expected to be paid. And then we had customers that went bankrupt—customers that I counted on to come through. And so I soon came up with this incredibly conservative approach that I wanted to have enough money in the bank to pay a year's worth of payroll, even if we didn't get any payments coming in. I've been almost true to that the whole time. We have about $10 billion now, which is pretty much enough for the next year."

RAM BEAU

Gates is also relentless. He has been playing poker in the computer industry, probably the most frantically competitive industry in the world, for over two decades now. A multibillionaire and still a relatively young man, he could retire any time he wanted. But he shows no signs of slowing down.

Many of those who were his peers when he started out have now bowed out or stepped back, including his former partner Paul Allen (he left Microsoft as a result of ill health when he was diagnosed as suffering from Hodgkin's disease). Although one or two of the original computer whiz-kids have tried to make a comeback, including Steve Jobs' return to Apple, Gates is one of the few to stick around in the war zone.

Many more have simply dropped out to write books, start new companies, or chill out. Not Gates— he wrote his book while holding off an antitrust suit and developing his response to the Information Highway. As he observed recently when asked about his plans to become a key player in Internet technology, "The fact is that most of our operating systems competitors seem fatigued. Fine, now we have got new competitors. It is always fun to be the underdog."[1] One thing that's certain is that this underdog bites.

GATES ON COMPETITION LAW

Critics complain that Gates is a past master at waylaying new product areas through the grandiose pre-announcing of its planned products. In effect, say many in the computer industry, by announcing its intention to market a new product, Microsoft warns off other software firms that fear a head-to-head battle—even though Microsoft may be many months away from launching its own product. This was one of a number of complaints leveled against Microsoft and investigated over the years by the Federal Trade Commission and the U.S. Justice Department's antitrust division.

However, Gates has always denied that Microsoft abuses its market position. In recent times he has mounted a strong defense of the company's impact on the PC market.

"The key role of competition law is to protect consumers and to make sure that new products get created and that those products are very innovative. And you can look at different sectors of the economy and ask, 'where is that happening very well?' No matter how you score it, there's no doubt that one sector of the economy would stand out as absolutely the best, and that's the personal computer industry. I don't say the computer industry at large, because you have to remember that before personal computers came along, the structure was very different. People were stuck. Once you bought a computer from Digital or IBM or Hewlett-Packard or anyone else, the software that you created only ran on that computer.[2]

"The vision of Microsoft was that all of these computers would work the same. The reason for that is that if you want to get a lot of great software, you have to have a lot of computers out there—millions and millions of them. So you've got to make them cheap, and make them so you don't have to test the software on all the different ones. The goal of the PC industry was to have every company competing to make the most portable one, or the fastest one, or the cheapest one. That would be great for consumers, and it would spark a big software market.

"Part of the PC dynamic is that instead of asking software developers to duplicate one another's work, we take anything that's typical in all those applications and put those features in Windows. So for things like connecting to the Internet, instead of everybody having to do that themselves, we put that in. That's been the evolution-graphical user interfaces came in, hard-disk support, networking support, now Internet support, including the browser.

"I think antitrust laws as written are fine. There are people who will debate whether they should be weaker, but that's of academic interest. When I come in to do business, I'm very careful to check with our lawyers to be sure we're steering a hundred miles away from anything that would be questionable. So it is somewhat of a surprise to find ourselves in an antitrust controversy. Thank goodness for the judiciary, which is an environment in which facts are tested and people can see if competition worked in the way it should and has been beneficial to consumers. There's no doubt in our minds where that is going to come out.

"In the meantime, we're going to be the focus of a lot of controversy because the filing of a lawsuit is a very big deal. You've got the government taking on that challenge and saying a lot of righteous things, and that's just something we'll have to be sure doesn't distract us from what we're really all about."

TAKE NO PRISONERS

Gates is a fierce competitor. In everything he does, he is driven to win. This makes him an extremely tough adversary. He makes no bones about this and talks openly about crushing competitors.

- *Leverage your market position. What Gates is unquestionably good at is leveraging Microsoft's market position to provide access to new and emerging markets. The reality is that if you own the operating system that runs 80 percent of the desktop computers in the world, that gives you a lot of negotiating muscle. This has aroused the interest of the Federal antitrust authorities, which have investigated Microsoft for alleged anticompetitive practices.*

- *Buy expertise. Gates' pragmatism also extends to buying his way into key markets. He has shown himself quite prepared to go out and buy the development expertise of other companies and plug it into the Microsoft machine.*

- *Keep personalities out of business decisions. For all his fighting talk, another characteristic of Bill Gates is that he does not allow grudges to affect his commercial decisions. The ultimate pragmatist, on many occasions Gates has fought a pitched battle with a rival for years, only to turn around and do business with them when it suits him.*

- *Balance risk against reward. Along with his analytical and detached approach to business, Gates is also a shrewd judge of risk. This is something he has learned as he's gone along. But while others who are risk averse have a tendency to delay decisions, Gates is only too aware that in the computer industry the speed of change is so rapid that not acting often carries the greatest risk of all.*

- *Be relentless. Gates has been playing poker in the computer industry, probably the most frantically competitive industry in the world, for over two decades now. A multibillionaire and still a relatively young man, he could retire any time he wanted, but he shows no signs of slowing down.*

NOTES

1   Kehoe, Louise and Dixon, Hugo, "Fightback at the Seat of Power," *Financial Times*, June 10, 1996.

2   Gates, Bill, "Watching His Windows," *Forbes* ASAP, 1997, taken from Jager, Rama D. and Ortiz, Rafael, *In the Company of Giants*, McGraw-Hill, New York, 1997.

4
Hire Very Smart People

The deliberate way in which Gates has fashioned an organization that prizes smart people is the single most important, and deliberately overlooked, aspect of Microsoft's success.[1]

RANDALL E. STROSS, BUSINESS PROFESSOR AND AUTHOR OF *THE MICROSOFT WAY*

B right as he is, Bill Gates does not try to take the credit for all of Microsoft's success. His willingness to acknowledge the talent of others in his field is crucial. As *Fortune* magazine observed: "Microsoft has been led by a man widely recognized as a genius in his own right, who has had the foresight to recognize the genius in others."[2]

It's a point endorsed by Gates. "I'd have to say my best business decisions have had to do with picking people. Deciding to go into business with Paul Allen is probably at the top of the list, and subsequently, hiring a friend—Steve Ballmer—who has been my primary business partner ever since. It's important to have someone who you totally trust,

Gates on hiring staff:
"I'd have to say my best business decisions have had to do with picking people."

who is totally committed, who shares your vision, and yet who has a little bit different set of skills and who also acts as something of a check on you. Some of the ideas you run by him, you know he's going to say, "Hey, wait a minute, have you thought about this and that?" The benefit of sparking off somebody who's got that kind of brilliance is that it not only makes business more fun, but it really leads to a lot of success."[3]

Gates himself does not suffer technological fools gladly. "I don't hire bozos," he says. In some quarters his attitude has been seen as elitist and has provoked criticism. But it has a number of positive effects. The company is able to recruit many brilliant students straight from college who are attracted by the prospect of working with the very best.

WELCOME TO SMARTSVILLE

"Bill Gates embodies what was supposed to be impossible—a practical intellectual," notes Randall E. Stross. "He consistently has sought out and hired the smartest individuals in the computer industry ... and always hires the brilliant if he can. Microsoft's principal assets, in fact, are the collective craniums of Bill Gates and his employees ... ."

From the start, Gates has always insisted that the company required the very best minds. Microsoft calls them "high-IQ people" and has always gone out of its way to attract the very brightest recruits. When required he will intervene personally in the recruitment process. If, for example, a particularly talented programmer needs additional persuasion to join the company, he or she is likely to receive a personal call from Gates.

"There is no way of getting around [the fact] that in terms of IQ, you've got to be very elitist in picking the people who deserve to write software ..." Gates says.[4]

Stars like to work wherever the best in their fields congregate. Sometimes, too, the top programmers will seek out for-

"In the software industry, a single programmer's intellectual resources, through commercial alchemy, can create entire markets where none existed before."

mer colleagues and persuade them to join Microsoft. For example, Gates recruited Charles Simonyi from Xerox PARC in 1981. Simonyi, who has been described as the "father of Microsoft Word," in turn helped persuade others to join. "In terms of hiring great people, how do we hire all these people? It's by word of mouth," Gates says. "People say it's great to work here ... ."

THE CAMPUS CULTURE

At Microsoft's specially designed headquarters at Redmond, Washington, he deliberately set out to create an environment that ideally suited the bright young people the company wanted to attract. With its simple aesthetics, open communal areas and green spaces, what it most resembled was the college atmosphere familiar to many of those joining the company straight from university. Appropriately enough, it was called the Microsoft Campus. (It was parodied in Douglas Coupland's 1994 novel *Microserfs..*)

THE ULTIMATE
INTELLECTUAL CAPITALIST

In the parlance of management theory, Bill Gates is the ultimate intellectual capitalist. From the very start he knew that Microsoft's key asset would be the caliber of its people. He has consistently recruited and retained the smartest programmers, often attracting them straight from college with little or no industry experience.

Randall E. Stross likens software to the Hollywood movie industry. "In the software industry, a single program-mer's intellectual resources, through commercial alche-my, can create entire markets where none existed before," he says. "Compare the cumulative worldwide gross revenues of the studio that captures the services of the next Stephen Spielberg to the rival who has to settle for a second-round draft pick. Differences separating the rewards generated by the top tier versus the second tier are geometric, not arithmetic."

In practice, most organizations still don't really value the talents and know-how of their employees. Those that do tend to focus on this element to the exclusion of the other dimensions of intellectual capital, such as rela-tionships with customers and suppliers, and the whole social fabric of the organization. These are all areas where Gates has led the way.

Carefully tended lawns surround wooded areas, and the low-slung buildings with white facing and dark green windows nestle in between. The orig-inal buildings were designed in the shape of an X to maximise the natural light inside. Unlike the open plan buildings popular elsewhere in the corporate world, each office was fully enclosed with a door, and was intended for one occupant.

This was a deliberate attempt to create the sort of solitude and privacy Gates felt was necessary to allow his employees to "sit and think" as he said he wanted them to. To ensure social interaction, the campus also included numerous cafeterias, which provided food at prices subsidized by the company.

In other respects, too, the culture has remained remarkably unchanged from the early days. Employees dress informally, they travel coach class, and use moderately priced hotels when they travel on business (including Gates himself). There are no status symbols such as executive dining rooms or fancy office furniture.

In fact the company has been built on an ethos of thrift. When some employees seemed to have lost sight of this a few years back and were felt to be taking advantage of the company's generosity, the culture reasserted itself. Employees were exhorted to shake off complacency: The company's success, they were reminded, had to be earned "one day at a time." Eating "weenies instead of shrimp" was the path to continued success.

Above all else, the campus atmosphere provides a pleasant working environment for Microsoft's most important employees. For those recruited straight from college it offers more comfortable surroundings than the traditional corporate headquarters. This is important because they are likely to spend a lot of time there.

CHARGE OF THE BRIGHT BRIGADE

Gates has said that the biggest factor affecting how fast Microsoft can grow has always been the availability of really smart people. To begin with he was able to recruit programmers he knew personally—"smart friends" as he called them—but as time went on this supply ran out and he found himself having to take on "smart strangers."

"The only real disagreement Steve Ballmer [one of Gate's right-hand people] and I ever had was when he joined the company. We had 25 people. He said, 'We have to hire about 50 more people to deal with all this opportunity.' I said, 'No way, we can't afford it.' I thought about it for a day and said, 'Okay, you just hire as fast as you can, and only good people, and I'll tell you when you get ahead of the sanity picture.' Here we are at 24,000 people now and still the key constraint is bringing in great people."[5]

Despite its exponential growth, Gates has always stoutly resisted the temptation to dilute the caliber of Microsoft staff, especially in the product development teams. He knew that attracting the best programmers would make it much easier to recruit others of the same caliber. Other companies might put new hires on probation, but Microsoft prefers to do the close scrutiny *before* they are hired. Getting it right at the start avoids additional cost later, including a drop in morale, that occurs when employees have to be dismissed because they aren't working out.

The company's credo on hiring people is that a mediocre new employee is worse than a disastrous appointment. "We're actually okay if the person doesn't come into work," Gates explained to Microsoft managers, outlining his hiring priorities. "But if you have somebody who's mediocre, who just sort of gets by on the job, then we're in big trouble."

The problem, as Gates sees it, is that a mediocre employee is hard to get rid of but occupies a place in the company that could be filled by someone brilliant. To avoid this, in the early days Gates insisted that the company employ fewer employees than were actually required to carry out the work. His formula was *n-minus-one*, where *n* was the number of people really needed.

This simple rule of thumb underlined a very clear message: Hire only the very best people because your team is never going to get all the bodies you want. To this day, Microsoft does not carry any passengers, and Gates takes a personal interest and pride in the recruitment of exceptional individuals, often interviewing them himself.

THE CAFFEINE KIDS

"I personally work long hours, but not as long as I used to. I certainly haven't expected other people to work as hard as I did. Most days I don't work more than 12 hours. On weekends I rarely work more than 8 hours. There are weekends I take off and I take vacations."[6]

Gates' famous stamina for work translates into a Microsoft culture that can best be described as "work hard, then work even harder." For many years, Gates regarded taking holidays as a sign of weakness. The Microsoft campus at Redmond is geared up to allow employees to work very long hours, with a selection of cafeterias providing subsidized meals. It is common-

It is commonplace for Microsoft employees to have pizza delivered to their desks so that they don't have to stop working while they eat.

place for Microsoft employees to have pizza delivered to their desks so that they don't have to stop working while they eat. The company even puts its hand in its pocket for soft drinks and coffee.

It has been calculated that Microsoft spends more than $8000 per employ each year on nonmandated benefits, with more than $715 a year per employee on beverages and food subsidies alone.[7] As one Microsoft employ told *Newsweek* in 1994, "Anything with caffeine is free."

Mike Tyrrel of Netscape can vouch for that. During his company's protracted negotiations with Microsoft he found himself doing business at what he regarded as some strange hours. "I had numerous conversations with them very late at night, from hotel rooms across the country and from my home. The phone would ring late at night and my wife would say, 'Don't tell me that's Microsoft again.' It was just the Microsoft way of doing business. I don't believe they ever really sleep."[8]

Whatever their nighttime habits, what Gates has created at Redmond is a unique working environment. It is at one and the same time a hothouse of creativity, and highly efficient at project management to ensure products are, with some notable exceptions, delivered on time. It is to the chagrin of rivals that the Microsoft development teams work as well together as they do. They have a voracious appetite for work and are virtually impossible to poach. According to *Fortune* magazine, this ability to hold onto its staff is one of the secrets of Microsoft's success. Gates achieves this, the magazine suggests, "by sharing the challenge to change the computer world with his staff. Microsoft staff feel more involved with their goal than other companies because they are led by a leader who is in the trenches with them." It is this ingredient that Steve Jobs brought to Apple in its early days.

Gates also has his own particular take on managers. He regards himself as an exceptional manager of people (even though some see his aggressive and sometimes impatient style as "management by abuse"). As a technical expert, he has little time for the notion of the generalist manager and expects Microsoft employees to combine managerial skills with other areas of expertise.

"The art of management is to promote people without making them managers," he said once. He has since modified that statement by saying it is more relevant to technical environments. His views on management, however, remain consistent.

"I really don't know the difference between a professional manager and anyone else," he says. "We're all professional, we work during the day and we get paid. Where are these non-professionals? I don't seem to see any around. We're not here to say 'I'm a professional manager, give me something to manage,' we're here to get the job done. So we don't actively distinguish between professional and non-professional managers."

What the company does do, however, is give its people very clear goals, tell them what is expected of them, and let them get on with it.

THE MILLIONAIRE CLUB

Microsoft has always paid its employees salaries that are lower than its rivals. Until recently, Gates himself took an annual salary of just $500,000. (In 1993, Microsoft paid its top five executives a total of $1.9 million combined, while head of rival Oracle Corporation Larry Ellison was paid $5.7 million alone.) What makes this possible is the company's long-term commitment to stock options—offering almost all staff an "option" to buy Microsoft shares at a fixed price in the future.

Through stock options, Bill Gates has made more people millionaires than any other entrepreneur in his-

THE MICROSOFT MANAGER

Microsoft has also put more effort than most into defining the role of managers.

"Anyone who has people reporting to them has the word 'manager' in their title," says Mike Murray, vice president of Human Resources. "We expect them to get more out of their people. We have found that there are three key drivers of a successful manager at Microsoft:

- *They make sure the group and every member in it have clear goal and objectives and performance measures.*

- *They must be very good at planning, the sometimes tedious process of figuring out the details of how to get there.*

- *They give continual feedback."*

tory. As one commentator observed: "Microsoft is singular in that its campus is a place unlike any other workplace in the world, at any other time in history, where several thousand millionaires, multimillionaires, and multibillionaires (two) continue to clomp to work each day."[9]

A Wall Street firm calculated that no fewer than 2200 developers in Microsoft's Class of 1989 became millionaires in just two years. The gamble has continued to pay off for successive waves of new recruits, even though some fear that the halcyon years when Microsoft shares doubled in price may be over.

The point to be remembered, however, is that as Gates is always reminding people about his own fortune, the sums are tied to the price of Microsoft shares. With the company's stock on a seemingly endless upward spiral, knowing when to exercise their stock options is the problem for Microsoft employees.

A joke inside the company is "there are a lot of $100,000 snowmobiles around here"—purchased for $2000 with money from selling stock options early before their value increased 50-fold.

Another key aspect of Gates' approach has been to consistently talk the Microsoft share price down. This is a sensible reaction to the wild fluctuations in share prices that can damage the prospects of an otherwise healthy business. As Gates is well aware, high-tech companies such as Microsoft are especially vulnerable to the vagaries of Wall Street, all the more so in the lead-up to the launch of strategically important new product releases such as a new version of Windows. To offset this effect, and in sharp contrast to most CEOs, Gates has spent many years talking down the prospects of Microsoft.

"We've always said that, given our long-term approach, this business will definitely go through cycles. There will be ups and downs. There haven't been any downs yet, but we are still sincere about saying that. We say our profitability, percentagewise, has grown at an unsustainable rate. We are always telling analysts, 'Don't recommend our stock. We sell software, not stock. Lower your earnings estimate, be more conservative.' It's not a long-term approach to promote the stock in any way. We are one of the most valuable companies in America, and I think it reflects people's optimism about the people here and what software can be. "[10]

By relying on the appreciation of share prices as the main element of compensation, rather than salaries, Gates has found the perfect linkage between performance and reward. As he notes: "We're using ownership as one of the things that binds us together."

What has surprised many is the number of employees who continue to work at the company even when they are financially secure beyond their wildest dreams. In fact, when people do leave, Microsoft's research suggests, it is usually not because they are rich enough to give up work but because the challenge has run out.

But perhaps the most telling test of the Microsoft culture is that so many of the original employees are still there. A lot of people in their late 20s and early 30s have become millionaires by taking advantage of the company's stock options. They could easily retire, but they don't. As one Microsoft manager puts it: "What else would they do with their lives? Where else could they have so much fun?"

HIRE VERY SMART PEOPLE

Gates has consistently sought out and hired the smartest individuals in the computer industry. This is a deliberate strategy and one that ensures the company attracts the highest caliber staff in its industry. Some people have accused Gates of being elitist, but he is one of the first entrepreneurs to truly understand what intellectual capital is all about.

+ *Hire only the very best. From the start, Gates has always insisted that the company required the very best minds. Microsoft calls them "high-IQ people" and has always gone out of its way to attract the very brightest recruits. When required Gates will intervene personally in the recruitment process.*

+ *Nurture creativity. At Microsoft's specially designed headquarters at Redmond, Washington, Gates deliberately set out to create an environment that ideally suited the bright young people the company wanted to attract. With its simple aesthetics, open communal areas and green spaces what it most resembled was the college atmosphere familiar to many of those joining the company straight from university. Appropriately enough, it was called the Microsoft Campus.*

+ *Don't drop your standards. Despite its exponential growth, Gates has always stoutly resisted the temptation to dilute the caliber of Microsoft staff, especially in the product development teams. He knew that attracting the best programmers would make it much easier to recruit others of the same caliber.*

+ *Work harder than anyone else. Gates' famous stamina for work translates into a Microsoft culture that can best be described as "work hard, then work even harder." For many years, Gates regarded taking holidays as a sign of weakness. The Microsoft campus at*

Redmond is geared up to allow employees to work very long hours, with a selection of cafeterias providing subsidized meals and even soft drinks.

♦ *Reward employees through stock options.* Microsoft has always paid its employees salaries that are lower than its rivals. What makes this possible is the company's long-term commitment to stock options—offering almost all staff an "option" to buy Microsoft shares at a fixed price in the future. Through stock options, Bill Gates has made more people millionaires than any other entrepreneur in history. Many of those who continue to work at the company are millionaires many times over.

NOTES

1 Stross, Randall E., *The Microsoft Way*, Addison-Wesley, Reading, MA, 1996.

2 Morris, Betsy, "The Wealth Builders," *Fortune*, December 11, 1995.

3 Schlender, Brent, "The Bill and Warren Show," *Fortune*, July 20, 1998.

4 Stross, Randall E., *The Microsoft Way*.

5 Jager, Rama D. and Ortiz, Rafael, *In the Company of Giants*, McGraw-Hill, Englewood Cliffs, NJ, 1997.

6 Jager, Rama D. and Ortiz, Rafael, *In the Company of Giants*.

7 Stross, Randall E., *The Microsoft Way*.

8 Wallace, James, *Overdrive*, John Wiley & Sons, New York, 1997.

9 Stross, Randall E., *The Microsoft Way*.

10 Jager, Rama D. and Ortiz, Rafael, *In the Company of Giants*.

Learn to Survive

Success is a lousy teacher—it seduces smart people into thinking they can't lose.

BILL GATES

In Microsoft Bill Gates has created a voracious learning machine. Learning, he believes, is the sign of a "smart organization," one that is continuously improving its internal processes. It is also the best way to avoid becoming complacent, and the best protection against making mistakes. His competitors aren't so careful. By capitalizing on the errors of others, Gates has prospered.

"Most of our success comes when we end up with a competitor who doesn't do things correctly—that's lucky. You're not supposed to work on a strategy that depends on other people's mistakes, but they've certainly made a lot."

Gates on others' mistakes:

"Most of our success comes when we end up with a competitor who doesn't do things correctly—that's lucky. You're not supposed to work on a strategy that depends on other people's mistakes, but they've certainly made a lot."

Gates' special talent is avoiding the bear traps that others fall into, while exploiting the opportunities that arise from their mistakes. In an industry where so many of the once mighty have fallen on their faces, Gates' track record is impressive—so far, anyway.

In many ways, what sets Gates apart from other leaders in the computer business is his focus on the business. Despite his incredible success—and the distractions of fame and fortune—Gates remains as committed to Microsoft as he was at the start. He combines an analytical mind with a real passion for the technology, which means that he is always scanning the horizon for the next big thing. This intellectual restlessness resonates throughout Microsoft. It keeps Gates and his people on their toes.

NO BUGS ON US

To date, Gates has shown himself to be remarkably resilient in a very competitive business. In large part this is because he sticks to what he's good at—software. At the very start when he and Paul Allen were setting up the company, it was Gates who persuaded his friend that the future was in software, not hardware.

With a few minor distractions—including marketing a Microsoft mouse—Gates has resolutely stuck to his guns on that point, insisting that Microsoft is a software company and should retain its focus on that market.

"Microsoft is designed to write great software," he says. "We are not designed to be good at other things. We only know how to hire, how to manage, and how to globalize software products."[1]

There is a rule, too, that any bugs identified in its software have to be immediately put right. The same approach applies to the way Microsoft's internal processes are organized. Under Gates' influence, the company has developed a voracious appetite for learning.

MICROSOFT U.

In Microsoft, Bill Gates has created what is probably one of the few genuine learning organizations in the world. The company's headquarters in Redmond, Washington, is organized along the lines of a university and is even called the Microsoft Campus. But the commitment to continuous learning goes much further than the physical environment.

In terms of establishing systems for retaining intellectual capital, Microsoft is way ahead of the game. Today, many of the world's best-known companies are attempting to introduce systems for managing knowledge (see The Learning Organization on page 82–83). But Gates has always emphasized the importance of fostering a culture in which knowledge is shared and retained.

Despite the apparently free and easy environment, Microsoft has strict rules controlling the way software is developed. In particular, Gates insists that Microsoft developers standardize their programming wherever possible, following the standards that have already been developed and documented. In this way, the development teams benefit from the work of their peers and can move easily between projects. The alternative, as other companies have found, is a prolifera-

tion of approaches, which leads inevitably to reinventing the wheel many times over.

The company is also fanatical about learning
from past mistakes. "I used to have this memo that I
updated every year called the Ten Great Mistakes of
Microsoft, and I would try to make them very stimu-
lating so people would talk about lessons for this company's future," says Gates.

"Many of our mistakes related to markets we
didn't get into as early as we should have. The constraint was always the number of people we could hire,
while still managing everything, and ensuring that we
could meet all of our delivery commitments. We were
always on the edge. We really pushed the limits of how
fast we hired people."[2]

Being able to bring new people into the organization quickly was a key factor in the way the company developed. By creating systems for documenting
knowledge, the company provided new recruits
instant access to what their colleagues had already
learned. Since relatively few people actually left the
company to join direct competitors, the risk of sensitive information leaving the premises was minimal.
One reason that Gates preferred to establish
Microsoft's HQ in Redmond, he said, was that the
close-knit community there meant "they couldn't
keep secrets in Silicon Valley."

LOOPING THE LOOPS

Gates also instituted a system such that those elsewhere in the organization provide constant feedback
to their colleagues. He is passionate about what he

calls "feedback loops," and these are built into everything that Microsoft does.

As might be expected for the world's leading computing firm, Microsoft has a highly sophisticated electronic infrastructure. Using E-mail, anyone in the organization can communicate with anyone else, including Gates himself.

One senior manager who left the company is rumored not to have checked his E-mail often enough.

"In a highly iterative business, where things change so rapidly, we often need to change course midstream, so we must have an efficient feedback loop. Our E-mail system, with its lack of hierarchy, ensures that everyone who needs to know about a problem is informed within 48 hours."

Gates himself is famous for replying promptly to E-mail messages from any Microsoft employee. One senior manager who left the company is rumored not to have checked his E-mail often enough.

The existence of feedback loops at Microsoft also gives rise to some concerns among competitors. One area of concern is the so-called Chinese Wall between the operating system development teams and the applications development teams. Owning the operating system that was the industry standard gave Microsoft's applications developers a huge advantage over other software companies. In theory, Microsoft was supposed to keep the playing field level by segregating the operating systems division and the applications division. This artificial division was called the "Chinese Wall." However, competitors have always argued that it is full of holes and that Microsoft's applications developers have inside information about the operating system that is not available to rival developers and vice versa.

THE LEARNING ORGANIZATION

The concept of the learning organization is based on the work of business academics Chris Argyris at Harvard Business School and Peter Senge of the Massachusetts Institute of Technology's Sloan School of Business.

"In the simplest sense, a learning organization is a group of people who are continually enhancing their capability to create their future," explains MIT's Senge, who brought the concept of the learning organization to a mass audience. "The traditional meaning of the word learning *is much deeper than just* taking information in. *It is about changing individuals so that they produce results they care about, accomplish things that are important to them."[3]*

Senge suggests there are five components to a learning organization:

♦ *Systems thinking—Senge champions systems thinking, recognizing that things are interconnected.*

♦ *Personal mastery—Senge grounds this idea in the familiar competencies and skills associated with management, but also includes spiritual growth—opening oneself up to a progressively deeper reality—and living life from a creative rather than a reactive viewpoint. This discipline involves two underlying movements—continually learning how to see current reality more clearly— and the ensuing gap between vision and reality produces the creative tension from which learning arises.*

♦ *Mental models—This essentially deals with the organization's driving and fundamental values and principles. Senge alerts managers to the power of patterns of think-*

ing at the organizational level and the importance of nondefensive inquiry into the nature of these patterns.

*♦ **Shared vision**—Here Senge stresses the importance of co-creation and argues that shared vision can only be built on personal vision. He claims that shared vision is present when the task that follows from the vision is no longer seen by the team members as separate from the self.*

*♦ **Team learning**—The discipline of team learning involves two practices: dialogue and discussion. The former is characterized by its exploratory nature, the latter by the opposite process of narrowing down the field to the best alternative for the decisions that need to be made. The two are complementary, but the benefits of combining them only come from having previously separated them. Most teams lack the ability to distinguish between the two and to move consciously between them.*

For the traditional organization, becoming a learning organization poses huge challenges. In the learning organization managers are researchers and designers rather than controllers and overseers. Senge argues that managers should encourage employees to be open to new ideas, communicate frankly with each other, understand thoroughly how their companies operate, form a collective vision and work together to achieve their goal.

"The world we live in presents unprecedented challenges for which our institutions are ill prepared," says Senge.[4]

Microsoft counters this criticism by inviting software developers from other companies to Redmond for briefings about the future development of its operating system. In reality, however, it is very unlikely that any such Chinese Wall could realistically be expected to work in such a competitive industry. For one thing, it flies in the face of the concept of the learning organization. In the real world the very notion of Chinese Walls is somewhat naïve. Microsoft has now appointed an ombudsman to monitor its practices for anticompetitive behavior.

CRASH TEST DUMMIES

There is one other crucial factor that has kept Microsoft at the top of its industry. Gates has always been willing to test software on customers. Beta versions of the company's software are offered to customers who are prepared to provide some feedback in return for advance knowledge of the new software. In this way, the company's developers get real feedback from the people who will use the final version of the software. Customers involved in beta testing tell the developers back in Redmond about any bugs or glitches they find, and offer input on the usability of the software.

In this way, the customer becomes part of the feedback process even before the product has been launched, something that speeds up market acceptance of new products. It is also a major factor in the speed with which Microsoft can develop and market new applications.

Critics argue that by releasing applications before they have been properly tested, Microsoft actually uses its customers as crash test dummies. However, many of the companies that get involved see it as a useful exercise to gain advance information about future Microsoft developments, and even to influence the final product.

Many high-tech companies have a vested interest in future Microsoft releases because the software and systems they produce are reliant on Microsoft software. They benefit from advance information from the company's development teams about the direction that technology is moving in—a factor that can make an important difference to the success of their own future products.

KNOW THYSELF

"If Hewlett Packard knew what it knows we'd be three times more productive," Lew Platt, chief executive of the U.S. computer giant, observed recently. And H-P isn't the only company keen to embrace the latest panacea for business success. Xerox, Unilever, GE, Unisys and Motorola are just some of the other serious-minded companies that are wrestling with the thorny issue of knowledge management.

Microsoft has been practicing knowledge management for years. It is linked to the broader issue of Intellectual Capital (IC). Intellectual capital, in turn, is usually divided into three categories: human capital, customer capital and structural capital. Human capital is what's inside employees' heads; customer capital has to do with customer relationships; and structural capital is knowledge that is retained within the organization and can be passed on to new employees. It is the third category that is the key to knowledge management.

According to Thomas Stewart, who has written widely on the subject: "Structural capital is knowledge that doesn't go home at night." It includes all sorts of elements including processes, systems and policies that represent the accumulation of the organization's experience over its lifetime.

Knowledge management is largely about trying to transform the other two types of intellectual capital into structural capital. The idea is that competitive advantage can be gained from know-how that can be captured, catalogued and made available to everyone. Through its continuous feedback loops and the standardization of programming code, Microsoft has always been good at knowledge management.

KNOWLEDGE MANAGEMENT STRUCTURE (KMS)

The Knowledge Management Structure (KMS) is a term put forward by Tom Peters as a development of the learning organization. The "new" firm must destroy bureaucracy but needs to nurture knowledge and skill, Peters says, building expertise in ways that enhance the power of market-scale units and that encourage those units to contribute knowledge for the benefit of the firm as a whole. Microsoft is made up of KMSs.

NOTES

1   Jager, Rama D. and Ortiz, Rafael, *In the Company of Giants*, McGraw-Hill, New York, 1997.

2   Jager, Rama D. and Ortiz, Rafael, *In the Company of Giants*.

3   Quoted in Napuk, K, "Live and learn," *Scottish Business Insider*, January 1994.

4   Senge, Peter, "A growing wave of interest and openness," Applewood Internet site, 1997.

LEARN TO SURVIVE

In Microsoft Bill Gates has created a voracious learning machine. It is, he believes, the sign of a "smart organization," and the only way to avoid making the same mistake twice. His competitors aren't so careful. By capitalizing on the mistakes of others, the company has prospered.

- *Stick to the program. To date, Gates has shown himself to be remarkably resilient in a very competitive business. In large part, this is because he sticks to what he's good at—software.*

- *Create a learning organization. In Microsoft, Bill Gates has created what is probably one of the few genuine learning organizations in the world. The company's headquarters in Redmond, Washington is organized along the lines of a university and is even called the Microsoft Campus.*

- *Create continuous feedback loops. At Microsoft, Gates has instituted a system such that those elsewhere in the organization provide constant feedback to their colleagues. He is passionate about what he calls "feedback loops," and these are built into everything that Microsoft does.*

- *Test your products on real customers. Gates has always been willing to test software on customers. Beta versions of the company's software are offered to customers who are prepared to provide some feedback in return for advance knowledge of the new software. In this way, the company's developers get real feedback from the people who will use the final version of the software.*

- *Know thyself. Today, knowledge management is all the rage with business school professors and management gurus. Microsoft has been doing it for years.*

6
Don't Expect
Any Thanks

Essentially, we have two choices. On the one hand, we can accept a characterization of Gates as the antichrist, Microsoft as the evil empire, its software as junk, and the company's success as rooted in deceptions, outright lies, legal trickery, and brute-force marketing. On the other hand, we can take the company at its own word that it has benevolently ushered in the personal computer revolution and that its market success is the just reward for the service it has rendered the public.[1]

RANDALL E. STROSS, *THE MICROSOFT WAY*

If there is one lesson that Bill Gates has learned the hard way it is that being famous and being infamous are closely linked. You can't expect to become the richest person in the world without making some enemies—and in the computer industry, Gates has more than his share of those. He has also attracted the interest of the Federal antitrust authorities, who have been investigating Microsoft for alleged anticompetitive practices for years.

At the same time, being incredibly rich and successful also brings its share of sycophants. These have ranged from politicians including Vice President Al Gore to Hollywood movie moguls who court Gates and his Microsoft executives. All those who beat a path to his door want to meet Gates or one of his right-hand people to discuss the digital future and the possibilities of collaborating with Microsoft.

In recent years, too, Gates has shown that he understands the importance of having friends in high places. Despite his on-going battle with the U.S. antitrust regulators, he has courted the CEOs of Fortune 500 companies, holding CEO forums in Seattle and other cities across the U.S. Recently he has also held discussions with the heads of a number of European companies.

Yet for all the publicity he attracts, Gates is fiercely protective of his private life, which he does not consider a matter of public interest. This is a naïve attitude on his part. Not only is he the head of one of the most powerful companies in the world—and one that, on a daily basis, is changing the way people live their lives, he is also the richest man in the world. When you add to that the facts that he possesses a celebrated intellect, his reputation for tantrums and his decision to spend millions on a mansion just outside Seattle, then it becomes clear that his every move is going to be closely watched by the world's media.

BILLION DOLLAR BILL

Bill Gates has a love/hate relationship with the media. On the one hand, he seems to enjoy the attention that greets his every pronouncement on the future of technology. On the other, he seems genuinely mystified by the negative publicity that Microsoft attracts.

In countries outside of the U.S., a visit by Gates is often afforded the same sort of attention as a visit by a head of government. Politicians love to be photographed in his company. Microsoft benefits from this publicity.

"The amount of press attention is not consistently linked to size: Microsoft and its chairman receive attention that exceeds all personal computer companies combined," notes Randall E. Stross. "Even though in 1996, Intel's earnings were exactly double those of MS—$3.6 billion versus $1.8 billion, ranking Intel seventh in highest profits of all corporations versus MS's position of 29th."

The somewhat overdue launch of Windows 95, for example, was one of the most written-about events in commercial history. The release of Windows 95 also points up the obvious downside—that the media is all over Gates when he gets it wrong.

MESSIAH OR ANTICHRIST?

The most startling aspect of the publicity that surrounds Bill Gates is its intensity. For some reason, to a large number of people Bill Gates has come to epitomize the sinister machinations of big business in a way that no other businessperson has ever done before.

In April 1996, for example, *Wired* magazine supplied its readers with a tourist guide to the World Wide Web entitled "On hating Microsoft." Every site listed was devoted to venting anger and other strong negative sentiments about Microsoft and Gates. One site proclaiming itself the "Bill Gates Fun Page" offered a photograph of the Microsoft CEO with two Devil's horns added to his head. Gates-haters were directed to choose from a selection of lethal weapons, including a knife, a hand gun, and an Uzi machine gun, that could be turned on his image by a simple click of the mouse. Weird as it is, this was just one of the more bizarre forms that anti-Microsoft sentiment has taken over the years.

Social historians may one day explain why so many people dislike Gates so much. For now, we can only speculate about what might be going on. The most obvious explanation is envy. A lot of people resent the fact that Bill Gates has made so much money and they have not. It may be that simple. But more likely there are a number of factors.

Is it pure coincidence, for example, that the rise of the Bill Gates as Antichrist movement mirrors the decline of that other U.S. bogey man, the Soviet Union? With the unravelling of the Russian communist empire, you could argue, there was a vacancy for a new evil empire. Who better to fill it than an incredibly rich and powerful computer nerd at the head of a global software company? Bill Gates, come on down.

Bill Gates is not the first mega-rich tycoon in American history to be vilified for anti-competitive activities. A century ago, the Texas oil baron John D. Rockefeller gained control of America's refinery business and oil pipelines. Rockefeller then leveraged that power into control of oil production. Critics of Bill Gates call DOS the equivalent of a pipeline and the control of the entire industry.

On the other side, there is an equally passionate, if much smaller, group that seems to credit Gates with almost godly powers. For these people, he is the golden boy, whose incredible intellect and visionary powers make him the closest thing the world has to a technology oracle. When Gates pronounces on the future—be it the likely convergence of technology or the spread of new software applications—there are plenty of people in high places who sit up and listen (notwithstanding the recent change of direction over the impact of the Internet).

CORPORATE BOGEYMEN

This is not the first time that America's thirst for a villain found a soft target in a hugely rich business tycoon. The reclusive oil baron John D. Rockefeller and J.P. Morgan, the king of Wall Street, both became bogeymen for the failings of the industrial age.

Teddy Roosevelt partly built the political career that took him all the way to the White House on trust-busting. He was the first to use the Sherman Act, the basis for the case against Gates, when he went after Morgan in 1902. The act had been drawn up 12 years earlier in response to the monopoly positions of Rockefeller's Standard Oil and others. In 1911, it led to the breaking up of Standard Oil into a string of smaller companies. Ironically, this actually made Rockefeller even richer. The same legislation was invoked years later against Ma Bell. In the 1970s IBM was also investigated, with some calling for the dismantling of Big Blue into a series of Little Blues.

Today it is Microsoft's turn, with Gates as Public Enemy Number One. As Randall E. Stross noted: "Essentially, we have two choices. On the one hand, we can accept a characterization of Gates as the antichrist, Microsoft as the evil empire, its software as junk, and the company's success as rooted in deceptions, outright lies, legal trickery, and brute-force marketing. On the other hand, we can take the company at its own word that it has benevolently ushered in the personal computer revolution and that its market success is the just reward for the service it has rendered the public."[2]

There are two sides to any story. Stross's research, which included access to the Microsoft archives, led him to

---

> *favor the latter explanation. Some people clearly dis-*
> *agree, believing the former to be closer to the truth.*
> *However, on one point at least Stross is right beyond*
> *any shadow of a doubt: The strength of anti-Microsoft*
> *feeling presents a very odd—and possibly unique—phe-*
> *nomenon. It is hard to identify any other businessperson*
> *who has ever provoked such deep distrust.*

If there is a lesson in all of this, it has to be that when you've got as much money as Bill Gates there is no way that you're going to please everyone—and its pointless trying. This he now seems to be realizing.

TECHNO TYRANT

On a personal level, too, Bill Gates has been described in less than glowing terms. As a child he had a tendency toward temper tantrums—a habit some of those who've worked with him say he hasn't lost. Certainly Gates does not suffer fools gladly.

"Time is very short, so if people are repeating things that I already know or if they aren't smart or didn't listen to something that I said with some precision, then that's not a good person for me to work with—they don't belong in this team," he once said. His own intellect makes him impatient with those who aren't as smart.

It has been remarked that Gates' social skills are not as developed as his other faculties. In reality, Gates is the product of his experiences as much as anyone else. A precocious and highly intelligent child, he went on to attend an elite secondary school before taking up a place at America's most famous university. He went to Harvard, he said, to learn from people smarter than he was ... and was disappointed.[3] The comment probably says as much about Bill Gates' opinion of himself as it does about Harvard. He dropped out of Harvard to start Microsoft with Paul Allen.

Gates has spent his whole life among very smart people and has a low tolerance for those whose intellect he does not respect. At company briefings he has been known to go ballistic, throwing things and shouting, "This is the stupidest thing I've ever heard of ...," a familiar phrase to people who work with him.

You could argue that if Gates behaves like a spoiled brat then he really doesn't deserve to be liked. But there is another side to Gates. He can be charming, if not quite charismatic. He has also shown on numerous occasions that he can be extremely patient when an important deal is at stake. The poker-playing days at Harvard have stood him in good stead. His cool, analytical mind makes him a better strategist than his rivals. He can also be extremely generous.

For example, on the day that Windows 95 "went golden"—i.e., no more changes would be made in the code before it was shipped—Gates sent a truckload of chilled Dom Perignon and several cases of whipped cream to the programmers who had been working around the clock. "You give 450 geeks champagne and whipped cream and it's an ugly sight," observed the team leader as his colleagues let off steam.

On one level, Gates is simply behaving like a brat when he throws his weight around. But then if you are the richest man in the world and a genius to boot, that's only to be expected. Journalists who interview him are lucky if they don't ask something that

Journalists who interview him are lucky if they don't ask something that Gates regards as a "stupid question."

Gates regards as a "stupid question." There are signs, however, that the techno-tyrant may be mellowing with age. Some say that marriage has calmed his temper, and that his friendship with the philosophical investment guru Warren Buffett is making him more relaxed about life.

BILL AND WARREN'S EXCELLENT ADVENTURE

When Bill Gates and investment sage Warren Buffett said they were taking a vacation together in China in 1995, many in the media thought it had to be some kind of weird publicity stunt. Commentators wondered what the world's two richest men could possibly have in common besides their cash mountains.

Buffett, in his late 60s, has described himself as a "cyber-idiot" who avoids investing in high-tech companies like Microsoft because he doesn't understand them. Gates is known to have a short fuse and to be impatient with people who aren't conversant with the ins and outs of software design. It is an odd friendship, then, but one that seems to have blossomed.

"We went to China for a lot of reasons. Partly to relax and have fun. We found a few McDonald's there, so we didn't feel too far away from home. It was also exciting to go and see all the changes taking place, to see different parts of the country, and to meet some of the leaders.

"China is a market that Microsoft had already been investing in. We've upped that a lot since then. As a percentage of our sales, though, it's tiny—well under 1 percent—and so even though it will double every year for the next five years, it's really only by taking a ten-year view that we can say it's worth the emphasis we're putting on it.

"Although about three million computers get sold every year in China, people don't pay for the software. Someday they will, though. And as long as they're going to steal it, we want them to steal ours. They'll get sort of addicted, and then we'll somehow figure out how to collect sometime in the next decade."

Gates and Buffet have been firm friends ever since that trip and have spent several subsequent vacations and weekends together. In 1998 they got together to give a rare public appearance, sharing the stage for a 90-minute question-and-answer session on their business philosophies. The event, held at the University of Washington near Gates' headquarters at Redmond, caused quite a stir: The line of buck-struck students stretched through the lobby and out the door of the union building in Seattle.

The billionaire buddies make an odd couple. Buffett professes to be computer illiterate, refusing to invest in companies he doesn't understand. Gates is normally dismissive of anyone who can't program a computer. Yet they get on like long-lost friends. On the occasion in question, the superinvestor and the cyber-tycoon invited 350 business school students to participate by asking a series of questions.

So what did this great meeting of minds reveal to the assembled audience? The $64,000 question—or, to be more precise, the $84 billion question, as that is what the CEO of software giant Microsoft and the head of the investment company Berkshire Hathaway are believed to be worth—was just how they got to be so loaded.

The two multibillionaires were surprisingly frank, without revealing anything. Buffett put his own financial success down not to his IQ but to "rationality." Anyone could do what he had done, he said with disarming disenguity; all they had to do was develop the right habits. That meant adopting the habits of those they admired and rejecting the habits of those they despised. He had turned down deals with people he didn't like, he said. The important thing was to enjoy what you did.

Gates agreed with both points. His own early habits, he admitted, had been formed by an early exposure to computers and the company of fellow computer fanatics. What he really enjoyed was solving problems. The Sage of Omaha and the Digital Sage were not giving away their secrets.

PEARLY GATES

Buffett and Gates are also in agreement about what they should do with their huge fortunes when they no longer need them. On the subject of inheritance, Gates is on record as saying he will not leave more than $10 million to any of his children. Buffett has been notoriously tightfisted with his three sons, and has told them to expect little when he dies. He says he will give 99 percent of his wealth to charity.

DON'T EXPECT ANY THANKS

If there is one lesson that Bill Gates has learned the hard way it is that fame and infamy are never far apart. You can't expect to become the richest person in the world without making some enemies—and in the computer industry, Gates has more than his share of those. What it has taught him is:

♦ *Don't let jealousy faze you. The most startling aspect of the publicity that surrounds Bill Gates is its intensity. For some reason, to a large number of people Bill Gates has come to epitomize the sinister machinations of big business in a way that no other businessperson has ever done before. His reaction is to defend himself with reasoned argument.*

♦ *Use media attention to market your products. Microsoft benefits from the publicity surrounding its famous founder. In countries outside of the U.S., a visit by Gates is often afforded the same sort of attention as a visit by a head of government. This gives Gates unrivaled access.*

♦ *Write a book about the future of technology. This is a somewhat risky strategy, but Gates obviously feels obliged to live up to his image as the computer visionary. Only time will tell whether the thoughts of chairman Bill are more than transitory.*

♦ *Hang out with the rich and popular. When Bill Gates and investment guru Warren Buffett said they were taking a vacation together in China in 1995, many in the media thought it had to be some kind of weird publicity stunt. Commentators wondered what the world's two richest people could possibly have in common besides their cash mountains. Gates and Buffett have turned out to be firm friends. Some of Buffett's popularity seems to be rubbing off on Gates.*

♦ *Give it all away, but not yet. On the subject of inheritance, Gates is on record as saying he will not leave more than $10 million to any child. He has yet to get into philanthropic mode.*

If Gates follows suit, he will be following in a tradition established by earlier American entrepreneurs. Henry Ford, John D. Rockefeller and Dale Carnegie all devoted large sums of money to charitable foundations in their later years. Cynics suggested that after a lifetime of business they were trying to buy popularity—and even a place in Heaven.

Bill Gates has been criticized for not giving more to good causes. In reality, though, he probably hasn't reached the stage in his life when such concerns weigh heavily on his mind; he's still a relatively young man, after all. If he decides later to set up the Gates Foundation, it is likely to focus on education, an area that he has expressed a desire to support through the provision of on-line learning. History suggests, however, that whatever he does with his money, he can rely on the media to criticize it.

NOTES

1   Stross, Randall. E., *The Microsoft Way*, Addison-Wesley, Reading, MA, 1996.

2   Stross, Randall. E., *The Microsoft Way*.

3   Wallace, James and Erickson, Jim, *Hard Drive: Bill Gates and the Making of the Microsoft Empire*, John Wiley & Sons, New York, 1992.

7

Assume the
Visionary Position

*The only big companies that succeed will be
those that obsolete their own products before
somebody else does.*

BILL GATES

Bill Gates is a new type of business leader. Over the years, he has repeatedly shown that he is the closest thing the computer industry has to a seer. His in-depth understanding of technology and unique way of synthesizing data give him a special ability to spot future trends and steer Microsoft's strategy. This inspires awe among Microsoft fans and intimidates its competitors. (Gates himself is dismissive of the visionary role. "Vision is free. And it's therefore not a competitive advantage in any way, shape or form," is a typical Gatesism).

But Gates also fulfills another important role at Microsoft. He is the custodian of the company's culture and values. Some companies such as Merrill Lynch have literally carved their values in stone (the

Gates on vision:

"Vision is free. And it's therefore not a competitive advantage in any way, shape or form."

company displays them in the entrance lobby of all its buildings). Others have documented them in books. Johnson & Johnson, for example, has its values written down in the *Credo* , which dates back to the founders of the company. Hewlett-Packard has the *H-P Way*, which you find written out by hand and pinned up next to the picture of the founding family. Microsoft has Bill Gates, the company's resident luminary and global IT guru.

SITTING AND THINKING

Today companies are moving away from hierarchical, command-and-control management structures. Leading the way are the new high-tech companies, which rely on knowledge workers such as software designers to carry out their work unsupervised. Microsoft was in the vanguard of this movement.

Gates says that he pays his people to "sit and think." But even more than the famously eccentric Microsoft programmers, Gates himself regards his role as that of the company's visionary. He is dismissive of the more mundane aspects of running a business, believing that his job is to chart the future.

"How do you manage the sales force and make sure that those measurement systems are really tracked down to the individual level to encourage the right behavior? I'll sit in meetings where Steve Ballmer talks about how he wants to do it, but that's not my expertise. How do we advertise to get these messages across? I sort of know where we are going long-term. I've got to make sure people are coming up with messages consistent with that future. But I'm not expert in those things."[1]

What Gates does regard himself to be an expert in is unraveling the technological past from the technological future. Gates' own talent is for understanding what's just around the corner. His great talent as a leader lies in his ability to inspire the people around him with the challenge of helping him to transform the computer industry.

In recent years, he has made his role within Microsoft more explicit, responding to his own brief command to "establish how things should get done." "I'm in the leadership role," he explains. "So generally that means working with the developers to ensure we're doing the right things, working with the right products and key customers."

RAM RAIDER

A criticism often made of Microsoft is that the company is not a great innovator, and simply raids the ideas of others, converting them into Microsoft products. Windows, Microsoft's PC operating system, for example, is still seen by many as an imitation of Apple's Macintosh software.

Microsoft has been described as "the fox that takes you across the river and then eats you."[2] But according to one industry insider, most of the criticism is sour grapes on the part of its competitors.

> Microsoft has been described as "the fox that takes you across the river and then eats you." But according to one industry insider, most of the criticism is sour grapes on the part of its competitors.

"Like the Japanese computer companies, Microsoft may

not be an inventor, but it perfects products," says Richard Shaffer, president of Technologic, an industry consulting group.[3]

Gates has also shown that he is good at fostering innovation, and he has created a culture that tolerates eccentric behavior from creative employees. One software designer at Microsoft, for example, filled his workspace with soft toys. Colleagues knew if they saw him clutching a teddy bear under one arm then he was having a tough day and should be approached with caution.

MANAGING CREATIVITY

Until recently, little was known about the actual management processes involved in channeling creative people. A recent research project carried out by John Whatmore at the Roffey Park Management Institute in the U.K. looked at how leaders of creative teams got the best from the special talents at their disposal.

Researchers put creative teams from fields including improvisational theatre, drug research, sport, theater, film and journalism under the microscope. "Creative people are often seen as difficult or impossible to manage," says Whatmore, "but it is clear that some people have a gift for getting the best from the talent available, and even for getting more out of creative people than they thought they had to give. It requires a different style of management—'a lightness of touch on the reins'."

The research indicates that people who excel at leading creative teams foster an environment conducive to inno-

---

vation and supportive of the aspirations of the individuals involved. They also have their own ways of nudging people to get their best ideas—or as one leader put it, of "tickling their thinking."

People who do it well have a number of common characteristics, the research suggests:

- They are often gregarious individuals, with the ability to stimulate ideas by expressing the same issue in different ways.

- They have the ability to read others, a skill that enables them to push the right buttons to get their best performance.

- They understand the interplay between creativity and criticism, setting up "creative tensions" between team members and providing constant feedback.

- They are adept at promoting social interaction between team members, often through informal meetings outside of work.

Beyond these personal skills, creative leaders have a vision of what can be achieved, based on a broad technical understanding of the field; they select team members with complementary differences, taking into account not just technical expertise but the mix of personalities and giving them a great deal of freedom; and they shield the team from external pressures from other parts of the organization.

Findings from the study suggest that effective leaders of creative groups do five critical things:

- They give members of the team a great deal of freedom.

- *They encourage people to approach issues as a team to maximize the creative energy focused on any given problem.*

- *They give support to individual members, particularly in the period after a failure.*

- *They give extensive responsibility to individuals, allowing them to decide not just how they will do a task but which tasks they choose to do.*

- *They shield the team from external pressures from other departments.*

But these elements are important to different people in different ways.

"Take freedom, for example," says Whatmore. "It's a wonderful metaphor for experimentation. There is the freedom to do what interests you; the freedom to start work at midnight; the freedom to back your own hunch; and, of course, the freedom to be wrong."

NERD INSTINCT

Gates speaks the language of computer programmers. He talks frequently about "maximum bandwidth" and even nicknamed one girlfriend "32-bit." This is both one of his great strengths as a leader and also one of his great weaknesses. Talking to fellow techies gives him an open channel of communication that allows him to inspire Microsoft employees to greater heights. On the negative side, however, his nerdy vocabulary and directness can make him seem inarticulate when he tries to communicate to the wider public.

(Asked by the American journalist Connie Chung if he regarded himself as a nerd, Gates replied: "If nerd means you can enjoy understanding the insides of a computer and sit in front of it for hours and play with it and enjoy it." What he didn't say, but could have, is that his nerdish hobbies have also made him the richest person in the world.)

Gates' own direct, slightly impatient manner and his unwillingness to suffer fools can also make him appear rude. On a good day he can be charming, but on a bad day he can be downright abrasive. At industry gatherings he can seem condescending, even patronizing, about the ideas of others. At internal meetings he is prone to outbursts—some say tantrums—if he doesn't like the way the discussion is moving.

"That is the stupidest idea I've ever heard," is a typical Gates line. Direct it may be, but it is hardly likely to make the person he's talking to inclined to volunteer more ideas. Steve Ballmer, a longtime Gates aide and friend for more than 20 years, is well aware of how the Microsoft CEO can come across sometimes.

"Part of Bill's style of presenting, clarifying and challenging ideas is to be very blunt, and a little bit dramatic and some would say a little rude," he says. "But he is a lot less rude than he was ten years ago."[4]

"Effective leaders recognize that the ultimate test of leadership is sustained success, which demands the constant cultivation of future leaders," says Noel Tichy of the University of Michigan.[5] Leaders must, therefore, invest in developing the leaders of tomorrow and they must communicate directly with those who will follow in their footsteps.

Tichy believes that being able to pass on leadership skills to others requires three things. First, a "teachable point of view"—"You must be able to talk clearly and convincingly about who you are, why you exist and how you operate." Second, the leader requires a story. "Dramatic storytelling is the way people learn from one another," Tichy writes, suggesting that this explains why Bill Gates and the like feel the need to write books. The third element in passing on the torch of leadership is teaching methodology—"To be a great teacher you have to be a great learner." The great corporate leaders are hungry to know more and do not regard their knowledge as static or comprehensive.

THE PARANOID PROPHET

It was another Silicon Valley visionary, Andy Grove of Intel, who coined the phrase "Only the paranoid survive" as the title to his book. But it could just as well have been Bill Gates. "The more successful I am," Gates noted, "the more vulnerable I feel."

From the very beginning, despite its near miraculous profit margins, Gates has always worried about Microsoft's financial situation. "Even though if you look back and see that our sales and profits grew by basically 50 per cent a year for all those years, what I really remember is worrying all the time. If you ask about a specific year, I'd tell you, oh that was an awful year, we had to get Multiplan [a financial spreadsheet] out and establish it, or that was the terrible year we brought out a Microsoft mouse and it didn't sell so we had a warehouse full of them, or that was the miserable year we hired a guy to be president who didn't work out."[6]

Even today, Gates says he is driven by a "latent fear" that the company could become complacent and allow itself to be overtaken by nimbler competitors. "Every company is going to have to avoid business as usual. The only big companies that succeed will be those that obsolete their own products before somebody else does."[7]

It is an indication of the nature of the computer industry that two such successful business leaders should subscribe to a business creed of perpetual paranoia. But it is hardly surprising given the speed of change within their markets. What these two modern business leaders recognize is that in their particular businesses, change is a given. The more established you are the more vulnerable your position. The problem for the market leader in an industry that is in a constant state of revolution is that you can be top dog one day and find yourself completely stranded the next because you didn't take heed of some change in direction.

The need to spot paradigm changes is most evident with high-tech companies. No one knows this better than Bill Gates. After all, it was precisely this sort of paradigm change that caught IBM napping and caused it to hand him the operating systems market on a platter, which in turn proved to be the dominant position in the software market. For this reason, Microsoft behaves at times almost as if it has multiple personalities, pursuing several different and even conflicting technologies for fear of backing the wrong horse. As its chief lookout and self-appointed visionary, Gates has the unenviable task of scanning the horizon for the next big thing. Sometimes even he can miss something big.

BETTER LATE THAN NEVER

Dark clouds appeared to be gathering over Redmond a couple of years back. Prophets of doom were predicting that the Internet could be Microsoft's undoing. Gates, they said, had been caught napping by the rapid advance of the Internet and how it would transform the PC software industry. Some even drew parallels with IBM, which lost its way at the beginning of the 1980s with the switch from mainframes to PCs. The chief beneficiary then was one Bill Gates.

A decade and a half later, the wheel appeared to have come full circle. Critics argued that Microsoft's illustrious leader was the last person at Microsoft to see the potential of the Internet for home users. This could have cost the company dearly. But fortunately, when the penny finally dropped for Bill, Microsoft had the resources at his disposal to play some serious catch-up.

Gates' revised view of the Internet:

"The Internet is not a fad in any way. It is a fantastic thing; it makes software and computers more relevant."

"The Internet is not a fad in any way. It is a fantastic thing; it makes software and computers more relevant."[8] Gates fans say his reversal of opinion and willingness to embrace a technology he once avoided actually show great strength of character, and are characteristic of the sort of leadership demanded in the modern business world.

There is even some academic theory to support this idea (or perhaps management theorists are simply

STRATEGIC INFLEXION POINTS

In his book Only the Paranoid Survive, *Intel's Andy Grove talks about "strategic inflexion points." These, he says, occur when a company's competitive position goes through a transition. It is the point at which the organization must alter the path it is on, adapting itself to the new situation, or it risks going into decline.*

"During a strategic inflexion point the way a business operates, the very structure and concept of the business, undergoes a change," Grove says. "But the irony is that at that point itself nothing much happens. That subtle point is like the eye of a hurricane. There is no wind at the eye of the hurricane, but when it moves the wind hits you again.

"That is what happens in the middle of the transformation from one business model to another. The irony is that, even though these are the most cataclysmic changes that a business can undertake, more often than not those changes are missed."

Peter Job, chief executive of Reuters, the news and financial information giant, is another practitioner who recognizes that the rules to the game can change very suddenly. The Internet, for example could be a new paradigm. "At those times," he says, "it's important to leave your strategy suitcase in the station and catch the train."

trying to unravel the leadership style of Bill Gates). Indiana University's Charles Schwenk contends that the call from management thinkers for strong visions could be the first step toward corporate totalitarianism.[9]

Schwenk believes that decision making needs to build from diversity of opinion rather than a simplistic statement of corporate intent. This requires "weaker leadership" and that "top management's vision needs to be less clearly communicated (and less strongly enforced) than the advocates of management vision recommend."

He points persuasively to the example of Microsoft's slow endorsement of the Internet. Originally, the Internet was not looked upon as fertile ground. Bill Gates' apparently all-encompassing vision did not include entering the Internet fray. Eventually, after much internal lobbying, Gates changed his mind and the company moved into Internet services. By traditional yardsticks this was an act of weak leadership. Visions are worthless if they are so easily changed.

Surrender is not in the vocabulary of the John Wayne–type leader. Think again. What if Gates was wrong? Should a single view of the future always prevail? Schwenk thinks not: "Without tolerance for eccentricity it is unlikely that any technique for encouraging the expression of diverse views will improve decision making in a firm."

Others would argue that the Internet example simply shows that even Bill can get it wrong sometimes. The fact is that, so far anyway, he has tended to get a lot more right than wrong. Only time will tell, however, whether he has the radar to guide Microsoft's progress in the twenty-first century, or whether age will automatically disqualify him.

UNIQUE FORESIGHT

"The question for companies today is how do you create strategy in the absence of a map? IBM didn't wake up one morning and take a stupid pill. It didn't have implementation problems in the 1980s; it had foresight problems ten years earlier."

So says Gary Hamel, visiting professor of Strategic and International Management at London Business School and coauthor of Competing for the Future, *the book that established the term "core competencies" in the business lexicon. Unique foresight, according to Hamel, is the key to strategy that works. The goal is not to predict what may happen but "to figure out the future you can make happen. It's about winning by changing the rules of the game."*

According to Hamel, companies don't need leaders with big ideas. "The next phase is to move to non-linear strategies," he says, "strategies that represent a quantum leap. They will not be created by the guys at the top of the company.

"Yesterday's visionary is today's straightjacket," he says. "Look at how Microsoft responded to the Internet. Bill Gates was the last person in the company to get it."

What companies need, he says, is to hear new voices. In many organizations the conversations about the future are the same people having the same conversations. Over time you get a lack of genetic diversity. It's ironic that in most companies young people who are its future are disenfranchised from the debate.

"Organizations need a hierarchy of imagination, not of experience. They don't need visionaries; they need activists."

ASSUME THE VISIONARY POSITION

Bill Gates is a new type of business leader. Over the years, he has repeatedly shown that he is the closest thing the computer industry has to a seer. His in-depth understanding of technology as a unique way of synthesizing data gives him a special ability to spot future trends and steer Microsoft's strategy. This also inspires awe among Microsoft fans and intimidates its competitors.

- *Sit and think. Gates says that he pays his people to "sit and think." But even more than the famously eccentric Microsoft programmers, Gates himself regards his role as that of the company's visionary. He is dismissive of the more mundane aspects of running a business, believing that his job is to chart the future.*

- *Adopt and adapt. A criticism often made of Microsoft is that the company is not a great innovator, and simply raids the ideas of others. But what the company is good at is recognizing the commercial potential of ideas and marketing them.*

- *Speak the language. Gates speaks the language of computer programmers. He talks frequently about "bandwidth", and even nicknamed one girlfriend "32-bit." This is both one of his great strengths as a leader and also one of his great weaknesses. Talking to fellow techies, it gives him an open channel of communication that allows him to inspire Microsoft employees to greater heights. On the negative side, however, his nerdy vocabulary and directness can make him seem inarticulate when he tries to communicate with the wider public.*

♦ *Watch your back. Gates says he is driven by a "latent fear" that the company could become complacent and allow itself to be overtaken by nimbler competitors. "Every company is going to have to avoid business as usual. The only big companies that succeed will be those that obsolete their own products before somebody else does."[10]*

♦ *Better late than never. Critics argued that Microsoft's illustrious leader was the last person at Microsoft to see the potential of the Internet for home users. This could have cost the company dearly. But fortunately, when the penny finally dropped for Bill, Microsoft had the resources at his disposal to play some serious catch-up. "The Internet is not a fad in any way," Gates said recently. "It is a fantastic thing; it makes software and computers more relevant."*

NOTES

1   Gates, Bill, "Watching His Windows," *Forbes ASAP*, 1997.

2   Wallace, James and Erickson, Jim, *Hard Drive: Bill Gates and the Making of the Microsoft Empire*, John Wiley & Sons, New York, 1992.

3   Kehoe, Louise, "Engineer of the Electronic Era," *Financial Times*, January 1, 1995.

4   Kehoe, Louise, "Engineer of the Electronic Era," *Financial Times*, January 1, 1995.

5   Tichy, Noel M., "The Mark of a Winner," *Leader to Leader*, Fall 1997.

6   Schlender, Brent, "Bill Gates and Paul Allen Talk," *Fortune*, October 2, 1995.

7   Kehoe, Louise, "Engineer of the Electronic Era," *Financial Times*, January 1, 1995.

8   Kehoe, Louise and Dixon, Hugo, "Fightback at the Seat of Power," *Financial Times*, June 10, 1996.

9   Schwenk, Charles R. "The Case for Weaker Leadership," *Business Strategy Review*, Autumn 1997.

10 Kehoe, Louise, "Engineer of the Electronic Era," *Financial Times*, January 1, 1995.

Cover All the Bases

*If you sit still, the value of what you have
drops to zero pretty quickly.*

BILL GATES[1]

A key element of Microsoft's success is its ability to manage a large number of projects simultaneously. Gates himself is the original multitasking person, and is said to be able to hold several different technical conversations simultaneously.

Gates refers to unused mental capacity as "unused bandwidth," and has deployed a number of techniques to ensure his own is kept to a minimum. These include posting maps on ceilings and taking copies of the *Economist* and scientific journals to read when he meets friends for lunch. His ability to juggle a number of different threads of conversation simultaneously has led to him being described by Microsoft insiders as "massively parallel."[2]

His ability to cope with a multitude of ideas at the same time is reflected in the company's approach. Microsoft is constantly exploring new markets and new software applications. This blanket coverage of the market protects it from missing the next "big thing."

MULTITASKING MAN

"We have a multiproduct strategy, so while we may have several individual products that have done poorly, when you look at the mix we've done extremely well," says Gates. "We also have lots of people working on any one question at any one time. To see it working you only have to look at our sales growth; it's almost a straight line going up."

During the 30-minute drive from his mansion on Lake Washington to the Microsoft campus in Redmond, Gates typically spends the entire journey talking on his mobile phone. Often, the conversation will continue for up to an hour after he has parked.

During the 30-minute drive from his mansion on Lake Washington to the Microsoft campus in Redmond, Gates typically spends the entire journey talking on his mobile phone. Often, the conversation will continue for up to an hour after he has parked.

The multimillion-dollar mansion he had built overlooking Lake Washington was also designed to be a multitasking retreat. Along with an underground car park that houses his collection of Porsches, the mansion has its own beach and movie theater. The dining room, described as a pavilion, can seat up to 100 Microsoft employees at any one time.

Part home and part office, it is a testbed for all manner of multimedia developments. Like something out of a science fiction movie or a James Bond film, it combines the latest in technology with luxury. For example, it is equipped with state-of-the-art computer entertainment facilities. These include high-definition screens and memory banks linked by fiber-optic cables, which enable Gates to summon up virtually any image in the world. All he has to do is type a subject on his computer keyboard and a picture appears on the screen.

IMMERSION THERAPY

One of the toughest challenges facing Gates is keeping up to date on technological change. With the pressures of running one of the most powerful companies in the world and the proliferation of technologies, trying to keep up to speed is a major problem. Gates is famous for his highly rational approach to problems. It is no surprise therefore to discover that he applies the same kind of approach to managing his own time.

In an interview published in *Playboy* magazine, Gates revealed that he had given up watching television, not because he disliked it but because it was not worthy of an allocation of his time. At his mansion on Lake Washington, Gates keeps a large library of more than 14,000 books—vital for a man whose intellectual curiosity can take him off in any one of a thousand different directions. He stays abreast of world news, he says, by reading the *Economist* from cover to cover. To ensure his time is used as productively as possible, he always leaves for the airport at the last minute. This habit led to his reinstating his own parking slot outside Microsoft's Redmond headquarters.

His intellectual discipline even extends to vacations. Up until a few years ago he didn't take holidays at all, believing them to be a sign of weakness. Now he takes several holidays a year and claims to have found a way to make them more productive by giving them a theme. A few years ago, for example, he went to Brazil and gave the holiday a physics theme. While he was away he read a number of physics books including *The Molecular Biology of the Gene* by James D. Watson.

In order to stay up to speed with new technologies, Gates will assemble a collection of the leading experts in a particular technical area and have them provide intensive briefing sessions. He calls them "think weeks" and they amount to immersion in a subject. During this period he will soak up information like a sponge. Gates loves to learn new things.

"Even in technology areas it's fun to learn new things," he says. "When I'm trying to find out where we are going with asynchronous transfer mode, for example, we have experts who come in and talk to me about those things. I spend two weeks here just doing 'think weeks,' where I read all the stuff smart people have sent me. I get up-to-date to see how those pieces fit together."[3]

OVERDRIVE

With one or two notable exceptions, the speed with which it has managed to get new applications to market has been a characteristic of Microsoft throughout its history, and one that has given Bill Gates an important competitive advantage.

What Gates realized from the start was that getting to market with a good product first is often better than getting there

What Gates realized from the start was that getting to market with a good product first is often better than getting there second with a great product.

second with a great product. After all, you can always refine the product and eliminate bugs next time around.

Critics of Microsoft have been inclined to regard problems with the first version of its software offerings as a major drawback. But from a strategic point of view, Gates is well aware that it is often more important to get the product out there than it is to get it 100 percent perfect the first time.

THE NIMBLE ORGANIZATION

Support for moving quickly comes from a prizewinning California Management Review *article by Stanford professor Kathleen Eisenhardt. Titled "Speed and Strategic Choice: How Managers Accelerate Decision Making," the article draws on the author's study (with University of Virginia colleague Jay Bourgeois) of decision makers in 12 computer firms in Silicon Valley. They found that the slower companies took 12 to 18 months to achieve what the faster companies managed in just 2 to 4 months.*

In the article, Eisenhardt highlights five major distinctions between the two groups:

1. *The fast decision makers swam in a deep, turbulent sea of real-time information, while the slower ones relied on planning and futuristic information.*

2. *The fast decision makers tracked a few key operating measures such as bookings, cash and engineering milestones, often updating them daily and scheduling as many as three weekly top management meetings to understand "what's happening." They also*

used a constant E-mail dialogue and face-to-face dis-
cussions, rather than the memos and lengthy reports
that typified the slow decision makers.

3. *The slow decision makers also considered fewer alter-*
   natives than their faster counterparts and minutely
   dissected each alternative, while the greyhounds con-
   sidered batches of options at the same time.

4. *The slowcoaches were "stymied by conflict" and con-*
   stant delays whereas the bullets thrived on conflict,
   which they saw as a natural and desirable part of
   the process; but the senior decision maker was also
   prepared to step in if needed and make a decision.
   The faster companies also relied on "an older and
   more experienced" mentor for advice, whereas the
   slow decision makers had no such advisers.

5. *Finally, says Eisenhardt, the fast kids thoroughly inte-*
   grated strategies and tactics, juggling budgets,
   schedules and options simultaneously. The slow kids
   examined strategy in a vacuum and were more likely
   to trip over details on implementing decisions.

SLEEPLESS IN SEATTLE

Gates is famously hyperactive, a characteristic that has
proved valuable in the computer business. He seems to
find it almost impossible to sit still and his habit of
rocking backward and forward when he is talking or
thinking is well-known within the industry. As a businessperson, too, Gates is restless, a trait that has helped
Microsoft avoid the sort of complacency that has
afflicted rivals such as IBM.

In what is quite probably the fastest-paced industry in the world, it pays to be constantly looking ahead for the next big thing. No matter how successful or rich he becomes, Gates does not let up. It must be a source of great concern for his competitors that Bill Gates refuses to rest on his laurels. Quite the opposite is true. There can be few more worrying prospects for his software rivals than the cold and unquestionable certainty that Bill Gates is relentlessly pursuing them with no sign of fatigue.

The fact of the matter is that Gates has one of the most severe cases of intellectual curiosity ever known. Even on holiday he consumes book after book just to quench his thirst for new knowledge. It's a characteristic that helps explain the enduring success of Microsoft in an industry where a great many once-successful firms have fallen by the wayside. It is one of the factors that makes him such a deadly adversary.

HEDGING HIS BETS

In recent years, too, it has become clear that Gates is looking beyond the U.S. for future opportunities. He is investing in the infrastructure of a number of different countries, pumping money into education, which many see as the next big growth area. Once again, Gates appears to be ahead of the game. He is hedging his bets on a global scale. It's a strategy that comes out of his unique view and synthesis of information. The Gates view of history in the postindustrial era is instructive.

"Which countries and companies are best prepared to take advantage of the information age that is revolutionizing society? When you think about it, 15 years ago this country almost had an inferiority complex about its ability to compete in the world," he says.

"Everybody was talking about how the Japanese had taken over consumer electronics and that the computer industry was going to be next, and that their system of hard work somehow was superior, and that we had to completely rethink what we were doing. Now, if you look at what's happened in personal computers or in business in general, or at how we allocate capital, and how we let labor move around, the U.S. has emerged in a very strong position. And so the first beneficiary of all this information technology has been the U.S."

In Gates' view, Silicon Valley was in the first phase of the revolution, but that doesn't mean its place is guaranteed in the second phase. "In places like Singapore, Hong Kong, and the Scandinavian countries," he notes, "people are adopting the technology at basically the same rate that we are. And there are a few countries that, relative to their level of income, are going after the technology at an even higher rate than we are because they believe so much in education. In Korea and in many parts of China we see incredible penetration of personal computers even at very low income levels, because people there have decided it's a tool to help their kids get ahead."

"The whole world is going to benefit in a big way. There will be this shift where, instead of your income level being determined by what country you are from, it will be determined by your education level.

Today, a PhD in India doesn't make nearly as much as a PhD in the U.S. When we get the Internet allowing services and advice to be transported as efficiently as goods are transported via shipping, then you'll get essentially open-market bidding for that engineer in India versus an engineer here in the U.S. And that benefits everyone, because you're taking better advantage of those resources. So the developed countries will get the early benefit of these things. But in the long run, the people in developing countries who are lucky enough to get a good education should get absolutely the biggest boost from all this."

COVER ALL THE BASES

A key element of Microsoft's success is its ability to manage a large number of projects simultaneously. Gates himself is the original multitasking person, and is said to be able to hold several different technical conversations simultaneously. He has also shown himself to be good at hedging his bets. The secrets of covering all the bases are:

♦ *Have your finger in lots of pies. "We have a multi-product strategy," he says, "so while we may have several individual products that have done poorly, when you look at the mix we've done extremely well," says Gates." We also have lots of people working on any one question at any one time. To see it working you only have to look at our sales growth; it's almost a straight line going up."*

♦ *Never stop learning. In order to stay up to speed with new technologies, Gates will assemble a collection of the leading experts in a particular technical area and have them provide intensive briefing sessions. He calls these sessions "think weeks" and they amount to immersion in a subject. During this period he will soak up information like a sponge.*

♦ *Less haste, more speed. With one or two notable exceptions, the speed with which it has managed to get new applications to market has been a characteristic of Microsoft throughout its history, and one that has given Bill Gates an important competitive advantage.*

♦ *Stay restless. Gates is famously hyperactive, a characteristic that has proved valuable in the computer business. He seems to find it almost impossible to sit still and his habit of rocking backward and forward when he is talking or thinking is well-known within the industry. As a businessperson, too, Gates is restless, a trait that has helped Microsoft avoid the sort of complacency that has afflicted rivals such as IBM.*

♦ *Hedge your bets. It has become clear that Gates is looking beyond the U.S. for future opportunities. He is investing in the infrastructure of a number of different countries to spread the risk globally, and pumping money into education, which many see as the next big growth area. Once again, Gates appears to be ahead of the game. He is hedging his bets on a global scale. It's a strategy that comes out of his unique view and synthesis of information.*

NOTES

1   Kehoe, Louise and Dixon, Hugo, "The FT Interview," *Financial Times*, June 10, 1996.

2   Stross, Randall E., *The Microsoft Way: the Real Story of How the Company Outsmarts Its Competiton*, Addison-Wesley Longman, Inc., Reading, MA, 1996.

3   Jager, Rama D. and Ortiz, Rafael, *In the Company of Giants*, McGraw-Hill, New York, 1997.

Build a Byte-Sized Business

Size works against excellence. Even if we are a big company, we cannot think like a big company or we are dead.

BILL GATES

Relative to its stock market valuation, Microsoft remains a small company. Internally, too, the company is constantly splitting into smaller units to maintain an entrepreneurial environment. At times, change is so rapid that Microsoft seems to be creating new divisions on an almost weekly basis. Gates also relies on maintaining a simple structure to enable him to keep his grip on the company. Whenever he feels that lines of communication are becoming stretched or fuzzy, he has no hesitation in simplifying the structure.

THE SMALLEST BIG COMPANY
IN THE WORLD

Although Microsoft now employs many thousands of people around the world, Gates has tried to retain the feel of a small company. "Even if we are a big compa-

Each time Microsoft grows too big, Gates splits it into smaller units with a maximum of 200 in each unit.

ny," he says, "we cannot think like a big company or we are dead. I manage the executive staff. Actually, on paper, there's only a few people who work directly for me. The whole thing is pretty collaborative. We talk about how my time can best be invested; when and how I should assist them to get their jobs done."

Observers say that Gates has been more successful than most computer companies, certainly better than Apple, at preserving the initial fun and excitement that made the company a buzzy place to work in the early days. "We enjoy working together—these are smart people and we have some very hard problems to solve," he says. "It's a competitive business, and they appreciate all the feedback I give them, including the negative feedback. We are all pretty well paid and we're all having fun—nobody cries too much."

Each time Microsoft grows too big, Gates splits it into smaller units with a maximum of 200 in each unit. The secret to the structure of Microsoft is that it is geared to the way that its famous CEO works best.

"When we were only 80 people, I knew when everyone came and went. I knew the license plate number on their cars and their individual projects. I was personally involved with everyone and reviewed every piece of code. Now it's all pretty indirect. We have more than 3000 people in the product development groups alone. Naturally I don't know everyone's names, but I know the key people."

DIVIDE AND RULE

Gates has developed his own unique system for controlling Microsoft. He also enjoys almost unrivaled power for a CEO. In the early 1990s, he reorganized the company to suit his own requirements.

At the top of the organization he placed the office of the president, which consists of three of his most trusted aides and himself. It is the commercial brain of Microsoft. Beneath this, the company has 15 grades of managers, with about 7 people at grade 15. Known as the "architects," they are the most senior of the company's software developers. Although they are better at writing computer code than he is, none of them has the collective vision that their famous leader possesses. That fact alone allows him to dominate them intellectually. He has been accused of bullying behavior, but he insists that how he treats people depends on them as individuals.

Of his top architects Gates says: "Some of them are kind of unusual; you really have to understand them personally. I'm actually friends with all my architects. When I work with the architects there is enough mutual respect that, should we disagree, I make the final decision and we move on."

This structure means that Gates only has to speak to one group of three and another group of seven people to control the company. It is his own version of divide and rule and it seems to work.

LARGE TEAMS THAT WORK LIKE SMALL TEAMS

Early in Microsoft's evolution, Gates came to the conclusion that the best software was created by small groups of developers. When the company decided to move, its Redmond Campus was deliberately designed to reinforce a small-group identity. To create the right environment, accommodations were provided in a series of two-story buildings that allowed team members to interact with their development groups on a daily basis.

Gates has also instituted systems that reinforce the effectiveness of the small-team mentality. According to MIT's Professor Cusumano, in Microsoft Bill Gates has created a special culture that fosters creativity, both individually and in teams, and at the same time meets commercial deadlines and demands.[1]

The Microsoft product development philosophy is labeled "synch-and-stabilize." This involves focusing creativity by evolving features and "fixing" resources, and doing everything in parallel with "frequent synchronizations." Exactly what that means is obscure, but clearly there is method in their madness.

What is striking about the Microsoft approach, says Professor Cusumano, is that the company is not the freewheeling ideas factory it is often portrayed as. In particular, he points out that the seemingly relaxed atmosphere is only one part of the picture.

Pizzas may be delivered directly to desks, but there is also a great deal of control—or discipline—at work. It may appear jolly and collegiate, but it is deadly serious. (Interestingly, Tim Jackson's recent book on Intel included similar observations of the chip maker.) For example, the scope and ambition of each and every project is carefully delineated.

The numbers of people involved and the time they spend on a particular project are also carefully controlled. Some rules are unbending—bugs have to be repaired immediately—to ensure that work is coordinated.

But, as Michael Cusumano points out, this is simply good project management, as applicable to software development as to any other business where product development is continuous. People are given responsibility and allowed to determine their own working patterns and schedules—up to a point. The boundaries are very clear and simple. People know where they stand, how the system works and what is expected from them.

MINING THE ETHER ORE

According to management writer and longtime resident of Silicon Valley Tom Peters: "Brain based companies have an ethereal character compared to yesterday's outfits, and that's putting it mildly. Time clocks certainly have no place. ... Barking orders is out. Curiosity, initiative, and the exercise of the imagination are in."[2]

No one epitomizes the switch to intellectual capital more than Bill Gates and Microsoft. Gates was one of the first to recognize that attracting and retaining the best computer programmers was the only way that Microsoft could remain on top. He has been mining the ether ore of his "high-IQ" knowledge workers ever since.

Key to his success is the fact that Gates is not greedy, and

No one epitomizes the switch to intellectual capital more than Bill Gates and Microsoft.

has been prepared to share the company's wealth around through stock options. According to one magazine he has made more people rich than any other person in history, inside and outside Microsoft.

THE RISE OF THE KNOWLEDGE WORKER

According to the experts, the switch from physical work to intellectual work—"brawn to brain"—is already well under way in the developed economies. Phrases such as "information age" and "knowledge workers" have been bandied around for some time.

The consensus among the experts is that intellectual capital, made up of knowledge and ideas, is now replacing physical capital, or factories and machines, as the key driver of wealth creation. Intellectual assets are now more valuable than those that have traditionally enjoyed pride of place in annual reports.

If intellectual capital is the new competitive imperative, then new ways of managing those assets are required. It is in this context that Bill Gates emerges as a powerful new leadership model.

Many of the world's biggest companies are falling over themselves to embrace the latest panacea for business success. Such is the corporate enthusiasm for know-how at present that a number of companies have created the job of chief knowledge officer to address this. Xerox Corporation, General Electric, and Hewlett-Packard are just some of the serious-minded companies now attempting to corral ideas and know-how. But Bill Gates has been doing it successfully for more than two decades.

UNLEASHING THE MICRO-SERFS

The way the company is organized also encourages entrepreneurial activity among Microsoft employees, and can act as a failsafe on Gates himself. Jeff Lill was part of the development team responsible for building an on-line service to compete with AOL, Prodigy and Compuserve, the market leaders at that time. The team felt that the Internet did not have sufficient priority within Microsoft, which had been slow in developing a response to the Information Superhighway.

When the project was presented to Gates, he was highly skeptical that they would be able to complete it on time. Despite his reservations, however, Gates gave it the green light and authorized additional resources so they could try. The team then took themselves off to an isolated part of the Microsoft campus. They declared the area the "Microsoft Enterprise Zone" and worked on developing the application in isolation from the rest of the company.

As Lill explained: "It was perfect. It was off by itself. Nobody was going to bug us ... I called it the Microsoft Enterprise Zone because it was this little crappy place, but great because we had the room we needed; and frankly, I liked being away from the rest of the campus. I wanted to avoid a big political situation, where everybody wanted a finger in our pie and needed to know our plans. I really wanted to be way out there on the side so we could get this done and get it launched."[3]

Mobility is important. Developers move from one project to another, jockeying for a place on the most exciting new start-ups. It is part of the Microsoft culture for individuals to earn their spurs in this way.

BUILD A BYTE-SIZED BUSINESS

Relative to its stock market valuation, Microsoft remains a small company. Internally, too, the company is constantly splitting into smaller units to maintain an entrepreneurial environment. At times change is so rapid that Microsoft seems to be creating new divisions on an almost weekly basis. Gates also relies on maintaining a simple structure to enable him to keep his grip on the company.

- *Create a small-team culture. Early in Microsoft's evolution, Gates came to the conclusion that the best software was created by groups of only a few developers. When the company decided to move, its Redmond Campus was deliberately designed to reinforce a small-group identity.*

- *Keep the feel of a small company. Although Microsoft now employs many thousands of people around the world, Gates has tried to retain the feel of a small company. "Even if we are a big company," Gates says, "we cannot think like a big company or we are dead."*

- *Keep reporting lines short. Gates has developed his own unique system for controlling Microsoft. He also enjoys almost unrivaled power for a CEO. In the early 1990s, he reorganized the company to suit his own requirements. He only has to stay in contact with a small number of managers to control the company.*

- *Share your wealth around. Through stock options, Gates has probably made more people rich than any other person in history.*

- *Create a meritocracy. There are virtually no status symbols at Microsoft. Respect has to be earned.*

There are no status symbols at Microsoft. Virtually all offices at the Redmond campus have the same furniture and the same dimensions—nine feet by twelve feet. This reinforces the egalitarian culture, eliminating potential squabbles about office size, but it also has another, more practical purpose. Standardizing the office size makes internal moves much easier to execute. This is an important point in a company where reorganizations are common. The design means that the facilities management staff at Microsoft can, if necessary, move 200 people into different offices overnight.

Only senior managers receive bigger offices: two nine-by-twelve offices from which the separating wall has been removed. Gates himself has a modest office and refused to accept a designated parking space for many years, until he realized that without it he could not expect to leave for the airport at the very last minute and still hope to catch his plane.

NOTES

1 Cusumano, Michael, "How Microsoft Makes Large Teams Work Like Small Teams," *Sloan Management Review* Vol. 39, No. 1, Fall 1997.

2 Peters, Thomas, *Liberation Management,* Alfred A. Knopf Inc., New York, 1992.

3 Wallace, James, *Over Drive,* John Wiley & Sons, New York, 1997.

10

Never, Ever Take
Your Eye Off the Ball

*Products are always gonna be obsolete so you'd
better enjoy doing the next version. It's like pin-
ball—if you play a good game, the reward is that
you get to play another one.*

BILL GATES[1]

G ates has been at the top of his profession for more than two decades now. In that time he has become the richest man in the world—not bad for someone still in his early 40s. Yet despite his enormous wealth and achievements, Gates shows no signs of slowing down. He says he is driven by a "latent fear" that he might miss the next big thing. He has no intention of repeating the mistakes of other dominant computer companies such as IBM and Apple.

I know very well that in the next ten years, if Microsoft is still a leader, we will have had to weather at least three crises." He says.[2]

THE THOUGHTS OF CHAIRMAN BILL

In recent years, Gates has felt the need to share his vision with the rest of us. His book *The Road Ahead,* which set out his view of the technological future, prompted some to wonder whether Gates' vanity was starting to get the better of him. Although the book generated a huge amount of interest, its message was not as inspiring or exciting as some had hoped.

The Road Ahead, *after all, concerns the obsolescence of pre-electronic media, yet it was delivered by a medium that would have been familiar to Caxton, credited with inventing the first printing press.*

Gates on decision making:

"That's my job and what's the point of having me here if I can't make my mind up."

Some commentators saw great irony, too, in his choice of the traditional paper book format to communicate his vision of the future: *The Road Ahead*, after all, concerns the obsolescence of pre-electronic media, yet it was delivered by a medium that would have been familiar to Caxton, credited with inventing the first printing press. Although the book was also published in multimedia format, readers reported that the original CD-ROM version was full of technical glitches, giving new resonance to the phrase "the medium is the message."

To be fair, Gates himself says he is wrong as often as everyone else in the computer industry. His argument is that he can afford to be wrong more often because he has so many projects on the go at any one time. "I synthesize a lot of information to get a broad picture," he explains. "So there are cases where I'll decide things a bit differently. But I'm the CEO and the technical strategy is in my hands. Sometimes I'm completely alone in my opinions if it's a technical question or a strategy problem.

"When it comes to a product decision there have been many cases when I analyze things in my own unique way. However if it is a business-type decision, rarely is my conviction sufficient to go it alone. Usually I'd take the time to get people to explain their views more clearly. That's my job and what's the point of having me here if I can't make my mind up."

DON'T LOOK BACK

"I have often thought that if Microsoft were a car, we'd have a very large gas pedal and a very small brake. There'd be a very large windscreen at the front to see where we were going, but no rear view mirror—we know the competition is right on our tail, so we don't need to look back," says Mike Murray, vice president of human resources at Microsoft.[3]

Fundamental to Microsoft's success has been Gates' willingness to keep his eyes firmly on the road ahead. "Looking in the rearview mirror is ... a waste of time, basically," Gates has said. The comment is reminiscent of Henry Ford, who said: "History is more or less bunk."

But Gates is well aware of the context in which he finds himself. He has a keen sense, too, of the history of both his industry and the march of technology

"I have often thought that if Microsoft were a car, we'd have a very large gas pedal and a very small brake. There'd be a very large windscreen at the front to see where we were going, but no rear view mirror—we know the competition is right on our tail, so we don't need to look back."

through the centuries. According to Randall E. Stross, author of *The Microsoft Way*, Gates is being disingenuous when he says that he never looks in the rearview mirror.

"He has looked back all the time—frequently, insistently, systematically," says Stross. "He cites historical examples whenever he discusses future strategy. He uses an historical perspective when he notes that in the commercial history of computing, no company that was the leader in one era succeeded in maintaining its position in the next one, and when he worries that Microsoft's place in the personal computer era may 'disqualify' it from maintaining its place in the coming network-centered era. Gates' historical sensibility saturates his analysis of the present and the future, but he simply does not label it as such."

INTO THE SUNSET

With his remarkable track record over the past two decades it is inevitable that people will ask what happens to Microsoft without Bill Gates.

If there is one issue more than any other that causes unease among Microsoft watchers, it is what will happen when Gates steps down. The transfer of power from one leader to the next can have a major impact not just on morale and business performance, but on the company's share price.

With his remarkable track record over the past two decades it is inevitable that people will ask what happens to Microsoft without Bill Gates.

Maintaining a supply of able understudies is often the best way to soothe concerns all around. Encouraging talented young managers from below, however, doesn't always come naturally to those at the top. Many will have had to fight off rivals on their way up the greasy pole. For them, potential successors may be perceived as a threat. As a result, it may be difficult for a new leader to emerge from the shadow of a powerful incumbent. Some people have called this effect the Thatcher phenomenon, after the former British prime minister.

But the thorniest succession issue of all involves a small group of business leaders, Rupert Murdoch, Ross Perot and Richard Branson among them, who are genuinely irreplaceable. These people play such a dominant role in their companies that they come to be viewed as inseparable from them. Of these, Bill Gates is probably the most difficult of all to replace. The difficulty then becomes: What happens to the business when they go?

Gates is dismissive of the issue: "The whole notion in the press of personifying a company through one person or a few people is a gross simplification, and it totally misstates the picture."[4]

But reports that Gates held discussions with his friend, the investment guru Warren Buffett, about his succession underline how sensitive the issue can be. News that its famous founder might be preparing to hand over the reins at the software giant could rock the company's share price.

Buffett's attitude to succession is typical of his approach to life. "I will keep working until about five years after I die," he quipped recently, "and I've given the directors a Ouji board so they can keep in touch. But if the Ouji board doesn't work, we have some out-

With so much of his personal fortune tied up in Microsoft stock, the one thing that's certain is that if and when Gates decides to stand down, he will have the interests of shareholders uppermost in his mind.

standing people who can do what I do."[5]

Gates agrees: "My attitude is a lot like Warren's. I want to keep doing what I'm doing for a long, long time. I think probably a decade from now or so, even though I'll still be totally involved with Microsoft because it's my career, I will pick somebody else to be CEO.

"Picking that next person is something I give a lot of thought to, but it's probably five years before I have to do something very concrete about it. If there was a surprise, well, there's a contingency plan."

Just what that contingency plan might be, however, he hasn't let on. With so much of his personal fortune tied up in Microsoft stock, the one thing that's certain is that if and when Gates decides to stand down, he will have the interests of shareholders uppermost in his mind.

THE DIGITAL SAGE

For obvious reasons, Gates generates a certain amount of awe among those who regard him as the predictor and architect of the digital age. To be fair, some if not all of his reputation as a visionary is deserved. History may judge him more kindly than do his many detractors and rivals, who say he is simply exploiting his monopoly position. Without Gates and Microsoft, it is unlikely whether the PC revolution would be as advanced as it is. Yet Gates is much too smart to rest on his laurels. More than any other figure in his industry he understands just what a treacherous road he's driving. After all, he's seen the cars in front drive over the cliff more than once.

"The technology business has a lot of twists and turns," he notes. "Probably the reason it's such a fun business is that no company gets to rest on its laurels. IBM was more dominant than any company will ever be in technology, and yet they missed a few turns in the road. That makes you wake up every day thinking, 'Hmm, let's try to make sure today's not the day we miss the turn in the road. Let's find out what's going on in speech recognition, or in artificial intelligence. Let's make sure we're hiring the kinds of people who can pull those things together, and let's make sure we don't get surprised.'

"Sometimes we do get taken by surprise. For example, when the Internet came along, we had it as a fifth or sixth priority. It wasn't like somebody told me about it and I said, 'I don't know how to spell that.' I said, 'Yeah, I've got that on my list, so I'm okay.' But there came a point when we realized it was happening faster and was a much deeper phenomenon than had been recognized in our strategy. So as an act of leadership I had to create a sense of crisis, and we spent a couple of months throwing ideas and E-mail around, and we went on some retreats. Eventually a new strategy coalesced, and we said, 'Okay, here's what we're going to do; here's how we're going to measure ourselves internally; and here's what the world should think about what we're going to do.'

"That kind of crisis is going to come up every three or four years. You have to listen carefully to all the smart people in the company. That's why a company like ours has to attract a lot of people who think in different ways, it has to allow a lot of dissent, and then it has to recognize the right ideas and put some real energy behind them."

THE QUICK AND THE DEAD

In the end, however, whatever the limitations of his vision, Gates remains the closest thing the computer industry has to Leonardo Da Vinci, the famous renaissance futurist whose drawings of fantastical machines became a reality centuries later.

Apart from his collection of Porsche sports cars and a $35 million mansion on the outskirts of Seattle, Gates is surprisingly restrained in his spending. One exception was his purchase of an illustrated manuscript by Leonardo Da Vinci for $30.8 million. This has prompted some to suggest that perhaps he sees himself as a latter-day Da Vinci—someone whose visions of the future are proved accurate in following centuries.

Unlike his hero, however, Gates is rooted in the here and now. His greatest attribute is his ability to combine technological innovation with a hard-nosed pragmatism. He also recognizes his own limitations— an unusual trait in such an accomplished individual.

"You have to be careful, if you're good at something, to make sure you don't think you're good at other things that you aren't necessarily so good at," he has noted. "I come in every day and work with a great team of people who are trying to figure out how to make great software, listening to the feedback and doing the research. And it's very typical that because

I've been very successful at that, people come in and expect that I have wisdom about topics that I don't.

"I do think there are some ways that we've run the company—the way we've hired people, and created an environment and used stock options—that would be good lessons for other businesses as well. But I always want to be careful not to suggest that we've found the solutions to all problems."[6]

Ultimately, though, it is Bill Gates' restlessness that more than any other factor explains Microsoft's success. He has always understood that the rapidity of change in his industry is fundamental to the competitive position of the company he created. To date, Microsoft has been faster on its feet than the rest of the pack. To maintain its position, its famous leader has never been afraid to abandon the past to pursue the future. More than any other figure in this century, Gates understands what the phrase *technological revolution* really means. He knows there are only the quick and the dead.

NEVER, EVER TAKE YOUR EYE OFF THE BALL

Gates has been at the top of his profession for more than two decades now. In that time he has become the richest person in the world—not bad for someone still in his early 40s. Yet despite his enormous wealth and achievements, Gates shows no signs of slowing down. The final lessons from the Gates school of business are:

♦ ***Don't try to explain.*** *Gates has felt the need to share his vision with the rest of us. His book,* The Road

---

Ahead, set out his view of the technological future, prompting some to wonder whether Gates' vanity was starting to get the better of him. Although the book generated a huge amount of interest, its message was not as inspiring or exciting as some had hoped.

♦ **Don't look back.** *Fundamental to Microsoft's success has been Gates' willingness to keep his eyes firmly on the road ahead. "Looking in the rearview mirror is ... a waste of time, basically," Gates has said. Yet he is well aware of his historical context.*

♦ **Plan your succession carefully.** *With his remarkable track record over the past two decades it is inevitable that people will ask what will happen to Microsoft without Bill Gates. In fact, the whole succession issue presents the man with the Midas touch with some-thing of a dilemma. With so much of his personal for-tune tied up in Microsoft stock, the one thing that's certain is that if and when Gates decides to stand down, he will have the interests of shareholders uppermost in his mind.*

♦ **Create the future.** *Gates generates a certain amount of awe among those who regard him as the predictor and architect of the digital age. To be fair, some if not all of his reputation as a visionary is deserved. History may judge him more kindly than do his many detractors and rivals, who say he is simply exploiting his monopoly position.*

♦ **Stay hungry.** *To date, Microsoft has been faster on its feet than the rest of the pack. To maintain its position, its famous leader has never been afraid to abandon the past to pursue the future. More than any other figure in this century, Gates understands what the phrase* technological revolution *really means. He knows there are only the quick and the dead.*

NOTES

1   Crainer, Stuart, *The Ultimate Book of Business Quotations*, Capstone, Oxford, 1998.

2   Schlender, Brent, "The Bill and Warren Show," *Fortune*, July 20, 1998.

3   Clutterbuck, David, and Goldsmith, Walter, *The Winning Streak Mark II*, Orion, 1997.

4   Jager, Rama D. and Ortiz, Rafael, *In the Company of Giants*, McGraw-Hill, New York, 1997.

5   Schlender, Brent, "The Bill and Warren Show."

6   Schlender, Brent, "The Bill and Warren Show."

How to Get Rich
the Bill Gates Way

With a net worth estimated at close to $50 bil-
lion, Bill Gates is the richest person in the
world. While this book was being written,
the value of Microsoft surpassed even that of GE,
becoming the largest U.S. corporation. Spectacularly
successful for more than two decades now, Bill Gates is
the most powerful of the new entrepreneurs, the King
of the Nerds.

(Asked by the American journalist Connie
Chung if he regarded himself as a nerd, Gates replied:
"If nerd means you can enjoy understanding the
insides of a computer and sit in front of it for hours
and play with it and enjoy it." What he didn't say, but
could have, is that his nerdish hobbies have also made
him the richest person in the world.)

How does he do it? A careful analysis of the way
Bill Gates runs Microsoft points to ten secrets of his
success. For those who want to follow in his footsteps,
here they are.

1. Be in the right place at the right time

In the era of the knowledge worker, technical know-how and creativity are the new corporate assets. Combine these with business acumen and a highly competitive nature and you have a rare bird indeed. Bill Gates is that rare bird. But a remarkable piece of good fortune carried him to an altitude where his special talents could flourish.

2. Fall in love with the technology

Bill Gates has had a lifelong love affair with the personal computer. From the very beginning, Gates and his partner Paul Allen could see that the PC would change everything. The two would talk late into the night about what the post-PC world would be like. They never truly doubted that the revolution would come. "It's going to happen" was an article of faith for the fledgling Microsoft, and they were going to write software for it when it did.

3. Take no prisoners

Gates is a fierce competitor. In everything he does, he is driven to win. This makes him an extremely tough adversary. He makes no bones about this and talks openly about crushing competitors.

4. Hire very smart people

Gates has consistently sought out and hired the smartest individuals in the computer industry. This is a deliberate strategy and one that ensures the company attracts the highest-caliber staff in its industry. Some people have accused Gates of being elitist, but he is one of the first entrepreneurs to truly understand what intellectual capital is all about.

5. Learn to survive

In Microsoft Bill Gates has created a voracious learning machine. It is, he believes, the sign of a "smart organization," and the only way to avoid making the same mistake twice. His competitors aren't so careful. By capitalizing on the mistakes of others, the company has prospered.

6. Don't expect any thanks

If there is one lesson that Bill Gates has learned the hard way it is that fame and infamy are never far apart. You can't expect to become the richest person in the world without making some enemies—and in the computer industry, Gates has more than his share of those.

7. Assume the visionary position

Bill Gates is a new type of business leader. Over the years, he has repeatedly shown that he is the closest thing the computer industry has to a seer. His in-depth understanding of technology and unique way of synthesizing data give him a special ability to spot future trends and steer Microsoft's strategy. This also inspires awe among Microsoft fans and intimidates its competitors.

8. Cover all the bases

A key element of Microsoft's success is its ability to manage a large number of projects simultaneously. Gates himself is the original multitasking person, and is said to be able to hold several different technical conversations simultaneously. He has also shown himself to be good at hedging his bets.

9. Build a byte-sized business

Relative to its stock market valuation, Microsoft remains a small company. Internally, too, the company is constantly splitting into smaller units to maintain an entrepreneurial environment. At times, change is so rapid that Microsoft seems to be creating new divisions on an almost weekly basis. Gates also relies on maintaining a simple structure to enable him to keep his grip on the company.

10. Never, ever take your eye off the ball

Gates has been at the top of his profession for more than two decades now. In that time he has become the richest person in the world—not bad for someone still in his early 40s. Yet despite his enormous wealth and achievements, Gates shows no signs of slowing down.

Last Word

What are we to make of Bill Gates? As Randall E. Stross, author of *The Microsoft Way*, puts it: "Essentially, we have two choices. On the one hand, we can accept a characterization of Gates as the Antichrist, Microsoft as the evil empire, its software as junk, and the company's success as rooted in deceptions, outright lies, legal trickery, and brute-force marketing. On the other hand, we can take the company at its own word that it has benevolently ushered in the personal computer revolution and that its market success is the just reward for the service it has rendered the public."[1]

There are two sides to any story. Stross's own research, which included access to the Microsoft archives, led him to favor the latter explanation. But whatever your views on his business practices, Gates cannot be ignored. In the history of business there has never been an entrepreneur so successful at so young an age. Nor has there ever been anyone who made so many other people so rich so quickly.

Computer visionary or ruthless monopolist? Messiah or Antichrist? Bill Gates provokes extreme reactions, of that there is no doubt. In the end, however, the reality is probably less fantastic. He is a very smart man, of immense energy and driven to win. But there is something of the Wizard of Oz about Gates. For all his undoubted intellect he cannot possibly live up to the size of the image he projects to the outside world.

For all the hype and all the accusations, one thing about Gates shines through: He is the greatest of all the computer entrepreneurs because he has both the technical smarts to understand what's just around the corner and the commercial smarts to sell it to the rest of us. This makes Bill Gates a very rare bird indeed. But what makes him so powerful is that he was standing there on the threshold of the PC revolution, to usher in the new era. There will never be another quite like him.

NOTES

1   Stross, Randall E., *The Microsoft Way: the Real Story of How the Company Outsmarts Its Competiton*, Addison-Wesley Longman, Inc., Reading, MA, 1996.

Index

best and brightest, 57-59
elitism, charge of, 57, 67
headquarters environment,
    campus-like, 59-60
"high-IQ people," 11, 58,
    67
intellectual capitalist,
    Gates as, 59
managers, view of, 64, 65
mediocre employee, dan-
    ger of, 61-62
n-minus-one principle, 52
salaries, 64-67, 68
"smart strangers," need to
    hire, 61
staff retention, 63-64, 67
stock options, 65-66, 68
work ethic, 62-64, 68
Human capital, 80

IBM:
    contract with to develop
        first operating system
        of PC, 10, 17, 19-22
    mistakes of, 20, 21-23
Innovation overrated, 37
Intellectual capital (IC), 38,
    59, 74-75, 80, 128-129
    categories, three, 80
Intellectual restlessness, 73
International strategy, 118-
    119, 120
IT revolution, 19

Jealousy as generator of neg-
    ative publicity, 87, 93

"Knowledge worker," rise
    of, 17-19
Knowledge management
    structure (KMS), 79-80,
    81, 128-129

Microsoft in vanguard, 97-
    98

Lakeside Programmers
    Group, 7
Learning:
    continuous, 74-75, 81
    from mistakes, 75
    organization, 77-78, 81
    components of, five, 77-
        78
    three sources of, vii-x
    experience, viii
    peers and colleagues, x
    training programs, viii-ix
Leveraging, 45-46, 52

Managers, role of, 64, 65
Media attention, negative,
    86-89, 93
Meritocracy, Microsoft as,
    130, 132
Microsoft:
    Apple, early advantage of,
        22
    mistakes of, 23-24
    biggest company in
        America, 9
    Campus, 59-60, 74, 81
    CD-ROMs, 39
    CEO power unrivaled,
        126-127, 132
    contract to provide oper-
        ating system for IBM's
        first PC, 10, 17, 19-22
    creativity, nurturing, 59-
        60
    culture, 335-36, 59-60
    cycles, 66
    domination of market crit-
        ical, 26
    egalitarian culture, 130